Sun Art of War Unveiled:
A Fourth-Dimensional Interpretation to Master Your Mind

GENEVIEVE TAN SHU THUNG

SANDHYA MAARGA HOLISTIC LIVING RESOURCES
http://www.holisticlivingannex.com

SANDHYA MAARGA HOLISTIC LIVING RESOURCES

http://www.holisticlivingannex.com
E-mail: books@holisticlivingannex.com

ISBN: 967-11301-0-0
ISBN-13: 978-967-11301-0-0

Cover Photography by Al-Haadi Abu Bakar

This book is dedicated to all who deeply yearn for the spiritual realisation of their unlimited Self. Marching forward on the path towards perfecting the Art of mastering one's mind, one discovers that it is this Source within one-Self that crates, sustains and destroys physical objective reality.

The Universe is in Your hands. There is no power from without, only within. Acknowledge that indwelling power, which you yourself, upon yourself, shall shower the beautiful light of Truth, granting you Liberation – Ultimate Freedom.

- Genevieve Tan Shu Thung

INTERNATIONAL BOOK REVIEWS FOR "SUN TZU'S ART OF WAR UNVEILED"

"This is a very thought-provoking and enlightening book. For someone who never studied religion or philosophy, it opened many paths of understanding and kindled a desire for further search of wisdom and fulfilment."

Anders Nelsson
Hong Kong Veteran Singer, Actor, DJ
& Founder of the Anders Nelsson Group of Companies

"This riveting book awakens our mind to human's true potential. It reveals simple strategies that will transform the way you think. You should get ten copies of it – one for yourself and nine to give away. It will change many people's lives."

Jonathan Quek
Wealth Coach
& Best-selling Author for "Why Gold? Why Silver? Why Now?"

"Excellent and compelling arguments from a very talented author who has clearly mastered the concepts about which she writes. The correlation drawn between the principles of Sun Tzu's Art of War and her own teachings is well-structured, succinctly characterised and thought-provoking at the same time. A wonderful read!"

Osman Johnson
Shadow Minister for Grand Bahama & Attorney

"Over 2,500 years ago, the great Chinese military strategist Sun Tzu handed down to posterity his inimitable treatise 'The Art of War.' Among his many pearls of wisdom is how one could successfully defeat an adversary with the inherent power of one's mind. Down the years, his thoughts continue to inspire and just as much mystify the world.

Genevieve Tan Shu Thung, a mindful seeker in her own right, takes a bold 'fourth-dimensional' approach in this book to shed insightful light in elaborating some of the salient yet elusive gems found in that timeless classic.

In lucid terms with scholarly presentation, Genevieve explains how Sun Tzu's strategic philosophy has become increasingly pertinent to modern times.

Her unique prose delivered succinctly in a compelling style helps the reader to comprehend and appreciate the very thoughts of Sun Tzu in a meaningful manner. She provides a gentle interpretation of the esoteric concepts envisaged by the illustrious sage.

As she unveils the true aspects of the soul-searching masterpiece of Sun Tzu, one fails not to see how the original strategy meant to gain victory on the battlefield could transcend into a win-win fait accompli for anyone living in contemporary times. Whether it is a corporate warrior or a harried housewife, Genevieve's book shows the way to a panacea that is already within one's mind's eye."

Charles Rex de Silva

Independent Editorial Consultant,
Former Editor-in-Chief for Borneo Bulletin
& Former Correspondent for the German Press Agency (dpa)

"This book shows the writer's capability in cultivating and exploiting the principles discussed in Sun Tzu's Art of War in a holistic view or approach whereby the great General's mastery of war is transformed into an art of winning the inner battle of conflict within oneself. The author's style of writing, coupled with her vast knowledge of holistic living as well as logical and interesting arguments managed to empower, provoke, inspire and influence the readers to learn from the great General's skills in order to win the enemies from within. For sure, this book can definitely teach you how to win against a struggle or confrontation, both externally and internally."

Akmal Syamsuddin
Editor for The Brunei Times
& Former Managing Editor for Jakarta Post

"Life is a battlefield of the mind. Genevieve's holistic approach in writing and explaining Sun Tzu's Art of War is wonderfully written to give a clear understanding on how a troubled mind can implement Sun Tzu's battle techniques in life."

Sukhbir Cheema
Journalist for the New Straits Times

"A brilliantly innovative application of Sun Tzu's classical treatise. Focusing upon the nature of the Self, it describes the psychological battlefield upon which life goals are fought for, then advises the reader upon strategies to attain them. Clearly set out with practical illustrations, having this book in your armoury ensures your goals WILL be achieved."

Maurice Thurman
Author & Retired Teacher

"You are what your mind tells you. Whether you are happy or unhappy with your current life, reading this book will definitely change the way you think. Every word you read will empower you and restore your inner strength to endure the journey in life to secure your goals."

Nicoleta Buru
*Founder for Fashion Consciousness Community
& Former Journalist with Flux (R. Moldova)*

"This is an excellent guide to deal with our inner conflicts. All naturopaths know that the mind influences the body and our actions. Even the best of medicine cannot confer us happiness and well-being. Genevieve clearly explains in her book, using the deep philosophy taught by Sun Tzu more than two thousand years ago, that the mind is the key to unlock man's infinite potential. This book will definitely enrich the readers' soul and inspire them to lead the best life they can."

Wong Eileen
Naturopath & Yoga Trainer

"Sun Tzu's classical war strategies are intelligently analysed and presented in this book to show everyone the way to achieve the success they have always dreamed of. A spiritual guide and teacher of Mental Science, Genevieve's teachings throughout the years to inspire people towards maximising one's potential in life are consolidated in this rare masterpiece."

Tey Sze Chze
Barrister-at-Law (Lincoln's Inn)

CONTENTS

Acknowledgments

A sincere 'thank you' to all readers, who are the very reason why this book has been written.

My deepest gratitude to Sun Tzu, the founder of the classic literary text of "The Art of War" that has helped so many individuals change their lives in so many different ways.

I would also like to express my humble reverence to those who have walked the surface of the earth, dedicating their lives to the spiritual upliftment of others and whose divine wisdom have transformed Mankind.

Thank You to my Beloved, the all-pervasive Universal Force of Nature that has inspired and aided the successful publication of this material.

My deep-felt love and gratitude to family and friends who have loved, encouraged and supported me in every way.

Last but not least, thank you to all my dearest disciples who demonstrated unwavering confidence in the principles I have taught during my spiritual lectures for the past many years.

INTRODUCTION

This is a new approach of interpreting the classical text of the Art of War by Sun Tzu, which will guide you to harness the power of your mind to live the ideal life that you desire.

Man is gifted with a great power - the mind. The mind is like a mad monkey, which is seemingly difficult to control, but it is still the most powerful instrument that we possess, which when conquered and disciplined will grant us liberation from limiting thoughts. The experience of reality is nothing but the ideas and beliefs that we hold within.

For too long people have been enslaved by the senses. They have given the power to other people to define their lives instead of writing their life story themselves. Most people believe that life is completely out of their control, a notion that has caused untold misery to mankind. The only panacea for suffering is for one to realise the Self and to understand the nature of the mind. Know that all power lies within. Nothing is impossible unto us as long as we believe.

Over the years, we have so many examples of people who have exceeded the limit of what most deem to be impossible. All success stories started with one single idea that the individual had persisted in. Before the Wright brothers invented the airplane, how many would have dared to dream of flying in the air? Before Alexander Graham Bell invented the telephone, how many would have thought that the people in the world today can easily connect with each other merely by keying in specific numbers on a piece of machinery? These are the people who dared to dream beyond the paradigm of what was seen by society as 'normal'. Though they were ridiculed for their 'impossible' dreams before they materialised, their unflinching confidence in their vision led them to their success. At the end of the day, the world still had to accept the fact that these dreams were not impossible after all. These examples prove to us that the creative power within is greater than any collective ideas without. We can still succeed even if our surrounding situation dictates otherwise.

The mind is a battlefield of conflicting thoughts. Since we reap what we sow, it is important to be selective of our thoughts and direct the mind to dwell only on those that will bring forth desirable experiences. Using the principles introduced by the world's most famous military tactician Sun Tzu from his Art of War literature, this book aims to acquaint you with the nature of the mind so that you learn to be the Master of your fate.

1 - 始計
THE ASSESSMENT

孫子曰：兵者，國之大事，死生之地，存亡之道，不可不察也。

Sun Tzu said: The Art of War is of fundamental importance to the State. It is a matter of life and death. It is the determinant of one's survival or destruction, and is therefore a subject that must be thoroughly examined.

The term *"war"* usually denotes two or more conflicting views or interests. In this world of duality, Man is constantly in battle with conflicting forces be it in his immediate surroundings or in his mind.

There are infinite states of consciousness. They are the plane of beliefs, which you have subjected yourself to live. Man constantly identifies himself with a state by saying "I am good or bad", "I am rich or poor", "I am beautiful or ugly" and more.

Between opposing forces, there can be only one that will take the throne. Similarly, only one idea can occupy your mind strongly enough for it to objectify as your surrounding reality on this physical plane. When you 'give *life*' to an ideal in your mind, the opposing idea will automatically be 'sentenced to *death*'. For example, you cannot convince yourself that you are rich and yet feel poor at the same time. Either one prevails. When you 'give *life*' to the belief that you are rich, you automatically 'sentence to *death*' the idea that you are poor. 'Giving *life*' to an ideal means to immerse or surrender yourself entirely to that one belief that there can be no room for another to exist.

The mind plays a crucial part in winning the inner battle within oneself. Vedic scriptures proclaim that the mind is the one responsible for the liberation (*survival*) or bondage (*destruction*) of man.

The mind is constantly moving, attaching itself to various states. It is important that man learns how to rise beyond the mind itself, but as far as man still lives in a physical form, the mind is a useful instrument, which when mastered, will liberate him from limiting circumstances.

When man is subjected to the whims and fancies of the mind, he shall be tossed and turned just like a sailor who is abandoned at sea. On the other hand, the man who has mastered his mind can be sure that his vision will come true until its very last detail. This is why it is important for you to learn how to discipline the mind so that you can be the Master of your fate instead of being enslaved by it.

故經之以五事，校之以計，而索其情，一曰道，二曰天，三曰地，四曰將，五曰法。道者，令民與上同意，可與之死，可與之生，而不畏危也。天者，陰陽，寒暑，時制也。地者，遠近，險易，廣狹，死生也。將者，智，信，仁，勇，嚴也。法者，曲制，官道，主用也。凡此五者，將莫不聞，知之者勝，不知者不勝。

The Art is governed by five factors, which are to be analysed and contemplated to assess the situation in the battlefield. These are:

1) The Path
2) Heaven
3) Earth
4) The Commander
5) The Rule

The Path is what causes others to be in complete accord with their ruler regardless of whether they live, or die. With that, there shall be no room for danger and betrayal. Heaven signifies Yin and Yang, cold and hot, and time or season. Earth relates to measurable factors; high and low, danger and security, wide and narrow, and life and death. The Commander denotes wisdom, trust, benevolence, courage and an unyielding nature. The Rule refers to recognising the hierarchy of the divisions in a system, each knowing who the Master is. These are the five factors known to every General; he who knows them is victorious, but he who does not, is bound to fail.

Before man is able to master his circumstances, he must first know the Self well. There are five factors by which man must contemplate on in order to assess his mental state.

"*The Path*" refers to the Universal Law; "as within, so without". It is a principle which states that everything experienced without is actually a reflection from within. The "*Ruler*" in Sun Tzu's text is none other than your Self, the inner being. You can choose for a mental state to be "*alive*", or sentence it to "*death*". The Path is yours. Regardless of your decision in selecting the Path, you can be sure that the dominant state that you hold within You is influencing the entire Universe, including all animate and inanimate matter. The state of mind that you dwell on is subjectively influencing others to form the very end result that you have decided upon within. There will therefore be no room for "*danger and betrayal*" because the Law is specific. As already mentioned in the above, you cannot assume a state of wealth within but at the same time, 'live' a state of poverty.

"*Heaven*" can be taken as a metaphor for subtle innate qualities. One is constantly transmitting subtle thought signals from within. Bear in mind that these signals you transmit are inviting the equivalent response from without. Hence, select the state which you wish to occupy wisely. The qualities introduced by Sun Tzu for the factor of "*Heaven*" indicate those that are directly linked to the Source. In the context of spirituality or Mental Science, the Source for man is the inner being.

On the other hand, the "*Earth*" factor signifies measurable aspects (in other words, circumstances) that result from man's perception using his five senses.

The Bible states that the kingdom of heaven is within you. The state that you seek to express on this physical plane can only be found within your consciousness (*heaven*). Remember that "*Thy will be done on earth as it is in heaven*" (Matthew 6:10). Whatsoever that you wish to experience and perceive with your five senses must first be established within. Step into that new state of consciousness and a new *Earth* shall appear for you.

Order is *Heaven's* first law. A *Commander* is one who exercises that order. Taking such a bold step in occupying a new state, you *courageously* assume your role as "*the Commander*" of your physical experiences with this newly found *wisdom*. By doing so, you *trust* the Source within You, knowing that the *Path* you have chosen will objectify itself in *good* time. A wise Commander knows that haste makes waste. Once you have planted the seed by believing in the reality of the ideal in your mind, let it grow "*for the vision has its own appointed hour; it ripens and it will flower. If it be long, then wait, for it is sure and it will not be late.*" (Habakkuk 2:3)

It is important to cultivate patience. When you have already experienced the state that you want to express without within, where is there room for impatience? Should there be any trace of impatience, it goes to show that you are yet to occupy that state by surrendering yourself completely to that ideal. Until then, that particular state cannot objectify itself in your immediate physical reality.

A Commander *never yields* to the whims and fancies of his troops, so similarly, never entertain doubt. Practice what people call unwavering faith. When the undisciplined mind begins to wander away, draw its attention back to the ideal. That is how man trains his mind. Let the mind know who the Master is. This brings us to Sun Tzu's fifth factor - the *Rule*.

It is important to recognise the *hierarchy* of *governing faculties* within the man: the soul, intellect, mind and senses. However, we must also know that these four, although seemingly distinctive from each other, are in fact governed by the same underlying universal force. This is the concept of Advaita (Oneness or non-duality) in Vedic scriptures: "*Ekatatma Sarva Bhutantaratma*" (Only one Atma, the Soul, dwells in all beings). We are all connected as an ocean of consciousness. Therefore, nothing is beyond our reach for we are all-pervasive. *Recognising the Master* is a crucial factor in ensuring discipline. The soul is the Master of the intellect, the intellect is the Master of the mind, and finally the mind is the Master of the senses. Knowing thus, the intellect can apply the timeless wisdom of the soul to properly govern and direct the mind towards worthy ideals so that they will objectify on this third-dimensional plane.

These *five factors* apply to every man (who is by nature, the *General* or Commander of his life), whether or not he exercises his power consciously or unconsciously. For those who are *aware* of these factors are *guaranteed to win* the inner battle, whereas *those who do not, are bound to fail.*

故校之以計，而索其情。曰：主孰有道，將孰有能，天地孰得，法令孰行，兵眾孰強，士卒孰練，賞罰孰明，吾以此知勝負矣。

Therefore, contemplate on these aspects to assess your present situation:

1) Which Leader has ascertained the Path?
2) Which General has the ability?
3) Who has conquered both Heaven and Earth?
4) To what degree is command and discipline enforced?
5) Which army is stronger?
6) Whose officers and army are more trained?
7) Is the reward and punishment system properly implemented?

Based on these seven criteria, I can forecast victory or defeat.

Whilst concentrating on a goal is crucial, the process of contemplation is of greater importance. This is also known as Self-enquiry. Throughout the process, you will develop the power of discrimination to help you master your senses and remain steadfast on your goal.

Sun Tzu has presented seven criteria to aid the process of contemplation to assess what the outcome will be for you. To illustrate my explanation, I will use the example of one's aim to graduate from university with flying colours.

"Which Leader has ascertained the Path?"

You must fist ask yourself, which part of you is winning the inner battle? With reference to my example given in the above, is the "I can" or "I cannot" part taking the lead? Which feeling plays a dominant role in your thoughts and feelings? The one that is most dominant establishes *the Path* towards materialising that experience in your reality on the physical plane.

"Which General has the ability?"

As already mentioned, you are the General of your life. We have two main distinctive characteristics of the mind; namely the conscious and the subconscious. Ask yourself if you are more attuned to your conscious or subconscious mind. The Universal Law operates on the "*as within, so without*" principle. Whatever you have impressed your subconscious mind with becomes your reality. Even when your conscious and subconscious are in conflict, the subconscious imprint invariably wins.

"Who has conquered both Heaven and Earth?

Which idea has conquered the concept of both Heaven and Earth? Listen to your inner talk. Does it point towards a successful graduation or are you anticipating failure?

The mind is a divine garden which you must consistently weed the weeds of doubt, fear and anxiety from. What you sow here is what you will be reaping. Your life is the exact reflection of what you have planted in this garden. That is how you will conquer 'Heaven'.

What about your physical actions on *Earth*? Do your actions show that you are prepared to embrace success or failure? Some people hold back because they are not convinced that the goal they have set for themselves is what they will be achieving.

For example, are you still reluctant to place that order to rent the graduation gown because you are unsure of whether you will be graduating or not? Have you bought the new suitcase that you are about to pack your clothes in with to take a short trip as a reward to yourself for having performed so well? All these actions draw a picture of your faith as to what is coming. "*As your faith, so be it unto you.*" (Matthew 9:29)

"To what degree is command and discipline enforced?"
How disciplined is your mind in remaining faithful to your vision? Do you recognise yourself as the Commander of your life or have you allowed external influences such as people's opinions and circumstances to sentence your experiences? If you acknowledge and assume your role as the Master, you will discipline the mind and not let it wander as it pleases to entertain the thoughts that are not the ideals which you wish to objectify in your reality.

"Which army is stronger?"
Is your inner conviction stronger than the opinions of the people on the outside world? When you and others say you can achieve something, you can. When others say you cannot

but you believe otherwise, you still can. However, the moment you believe you cannot, you will definitely fail!

"Whose officers and army are more trained?"

It is important to train yourself to develop the practice of turning to your subconscious for any given situation.

Social order has been established to provide a guideline for the acceptable ways of thinking, relating and behaving. However, they are not conclusive. When any of these concepts do not resonate with your heart, train yourself to tune into your subconscious mind to set a new pattern.

For example, you may like to be a successful musician because music is your passion but society (especially Asians) simply sees such career track as unfeasible and not practical. For most Asian parents, jobs that do not require you to sit in the office all day are just not good enough to be the source of reliable income. So, that is the collective concept that society has come up with. These concepts have been established to lure you into adhering to the standards set by others.

Now, you can either choose to conform to their ideas, or you can train yourself to take charge by relying solely on the power of your subconscious mind to determine the 'end result'.

"Is the reward and punishment system properly implemented?"

You have to use your discrimination wisely to determine which ideas be allowed to 'live', and those that should be 'sentenced to death' within you. This is the reward and punishment system.

"Based on these seven criteria, I can forecast victory or defeat."
With these seven criteria, you will have an honest evaluation of what to expect as the final outcome. From your answers, you will already know whether or not your desire will objectify itself on this physical plane. If you do not like the answer, then change your ways now!

將聽吾計，用之必勝，留之；將不聽吾計，用之必敗，去之。

A General who adheres to my guidance is promised victory; retain him. He who ignores it is definitely bound to fail; dismiss him!

If you heed all the criteria that have been proposed in the above, you are bound to be successful in the journey towards mastering your mind, and ultimately, your life. Continue without ceasing.

However, if you have been leading your life the other way round, allowing others to be in control of your actions and reactions, you are *bound to face failure* in all your endeavours. Start thinking of *dismissing* this version of 'you' who is currently in power and replace it with the 'you' who will be the one solely in charge of your life from now onwards.

計利以聽，乃為之勢，以佐其外；勢者，因利而制權也。

Whilst you benefit from what you have heard from me, you should also do your part in assessing the situation and implementing appropriate favourable plans accordingly.

During your journey in life, there are many unexpected situations that may occur. Opportunities for something better may present themselves any time and it is up to you to use the power of discrimination wisely to determine what is best.

For example, you have in mind to enjoy a wonderful time with a special someone. So, you plan for the both of you to dine in one particular restaurant because that is the best restaurant you know. You maintain a high spirit for days, imagining the perfect evening to your very best as you look forward to spend time with your beloved. However, when the day finally comes, your partner suddenly calls you to convey the message that she somehow got delayed elsewhere and it will take her a few hours to reach the restaurant.

You are now faced with two choices. You can either continue to wait for her where you are (at the same restaurant) or to dismiss the plan of dining there and meet up with her somewhere else instead. These circumstances are unexpected but it may be an opportunity for something better. After all, you did maintain a 'high' spirit of positivism about having a good time with each other. That was the crux of your desire.

So, perhaps you decide to opt for the latter choice. Nearby the new meeting point, you then discover that there are better places around the area for both of you to have fun. You also come across a better restaurant than the one you initially wanted to dine in. The whole evening unfolds one by one 'perfectly' just for you.

Therefore, the moral of the story here is that despite the fact that you may have an initial plan as to how you will work towards your goal, remember to never be too rigid that you do not give something else a chance that may eventually turn out to be better for you. Remember to continuously assess the situation and develop on the idea accordingly during the course of materialising any ideal.

兵者，詭道也。故能而示之不能，用而示之不用，近而示之遠，遠而示之近。

Warfare is based on deception:
When you are able to attack, appear unable;
When you are active, appear inactive;
When you are near, appear far;
When you are far, appear near;

Deception is indicative of something of dubious value. The way to exercise your mind into manifesting the life you envision, which is still yet to objectify in your current physical reality, is to convince the mind that it already exists. You are to reject any circumstances that your five senses perceive as being true if they do not conform to your inner vision. Instead, experience with your five inner senses that you already possess the very thing you desire. Manipulate your five senses and steer them towards perceiving your goal as though they have already materialised.

When you have convinced yourself that that is so, stop desiring because there cannot be any room for desire when you already have it. That is why ancient Indian sages have proclaimed that life with desires is man, whereas a life without desires is verily God.

Whilst anticipating for a particular outcome to objectify itself, the current surrounding should be perceived as being *far* away. On the other hand, your goal that is still yet to materialise (appearing far away from you) should be experienced as already being *near* to you. Do not chase after it. Be confident that it will make its way to you.

利而誘之，亂而取之，實而備之，強而避之；

Lure the enemy and take advantage. Create disorder on the enemy's side, and then eliminate them. If he is secured at all points, be prepared. If the enemy is strong, avoid them.

Have you ever heard that the worst enemy is yourself? An undisciplined mind is undoubtedly your worst enemy!

The term "*luring*" is evocative for the process of diverting one's attention to something else. This can be applied to the practice of spirituality and Mental Science in that one can direct the mind, which may currently be focused on negative circumstances, to focus on the ideal that you have set for yourself instead. Lure the undisciplined mind right to where it should belong - on the goal.

Sun Tzu goes on to suggest that the warrior should "*create disorder on the enemy's side and eliminate them*". Disorder is often a result of an opposing force. It is suggestive of unsettledness resulting from a challenge. Anything that is not in order cannot possess great power. That is Law. Disorder is caused by conflicting views or interests. Therefore, challenge a doubting mind with faith, and you shall eliminate doubt from your thought system.

Do not let your senses control you. We have already covered the chain of command earlier. You now know that recognition of the Master is a crucial factor in ensuring discipline. You are the Master and you are the sole determinant of what the mind should focus on to objectify an ideal, and not the other way round!

When the senses start to forget who the Master is, put them back to their rightful place by reprimanding the negative thoughts (Sun Tzu's *reward and punishment* factor) they have conjured in your mind. Your Self has to be the guide to steer the mind towards the thoughts that you would like it to entertain. With that, you shall eliminate any form of insubordination of both the mind and senses by resisting to give in to them.

As in any battlefield (external or internal), *preparation* is vital. You must always remain alert and on the watch out for any possible factors that may weaken your resolution in realising a goal.

Avoiding the enemy when *they are strong* does not imply running away from the opposition. It refers to the needless 'physical confrontation' with others to manifest an ideal. Your surrounding environment may deny the existence of that ideal as having already materialised, but so what? Turn away from this image and focus within that it is already done.

怒而撓之，卑而驕之，佚而勞之，親而離之。

If the enemy has a temper, seek to irritate him. Pretend to be weak so that he may be arrogant. If the enemy is at ease, toil them. If they are united, divide them.

Here, Sun Tzu implies the need to take advantage of every possible situation, giving your 'enemy' *no rest*. "*Temper*" and "*arrogance*" are indicative of weakness. Hence, search for possible weaknesses in the mind (e.g. doubt, fear and anxiety) and eradicate them! Amidst any adversity, turn it into an opportunity for a greater benefit!

Do not let the 'enemy' (negative thoughts and habits) to be *at ease* that they begin to sink deeply into your thought system. Challenge them whenever you can. If they appear too strong for you to overcome them as a whole, then, *divide them* into smaller units and work on them one-by-one until they are completely eradicated from your consciousness.

攻其無備，出其不意，此兵家之勝，不可先傳也。

Attack the enemy when he is unprepared. Appear at places where you are not expected. This military strategy which promises victory should not be divulged beforehand.

This is by far, one of the most important reminders that one must learn in the course of gaining mastery over your circumstances.

In the Bible's Old Testament, Joshua is promised that *"every place that the sole of (his) foot shall tread upon"* becomes his. In Mental Science, wherever you stand (earlier indicated by *the Path* you have chosen) in your mind, it shall materialise.

The Bible goes on to describe how Joshua desires the state called Jericho but is barred by its impassable walls. He therefore employs the services of a harlot, who is also a spy by the name of Rahab (translated as the Spirit) to enter the city. A 'harlot' is one who grants you anything that you ask for. This calls for you to tune within your Self when you wish to bring something to pass. A 'spy' is able to travel secretly without anyone detecting him or her. Therefore, when you tune your thoughts within your Self, there is no one who will be able to tell where you are mentally dwelling.

By doing so, you can choose the mental image that you would like to see objectify in your current circumstances. This would be the same as *"attacking the enemy"*, which is the current circumstances that deny you of your ideal, *"when he is unprepared"*.

Once you have closed your eyes, you can assume to be anywhere and anyone you want to be. Although you remain physically bound to the body on this third-dimensional plane, it does not prevent you from travelling even thousands of miles away mentally in the fourth-dimension. This is exactly what happens during a meditation session. One breaks free from the limitation of the body with the process of visualisation and it is guaranteed that no one can ever find out your mental dwelling place. You will then have *"appeared at places"* where you are *"not expected"*.

Rahab is specifically directed not to hop from house to house. Instead, she is to make her way to the upper room of the house which she has entered at the heart of the city. She is to remain there as the walls of Jericho crumble. This story is metaphorically true. Control the mind. Do not allow it to hop aimlessly all over the place. Direct the mind to focus on the very goal you desire to materialise on this physical plane. Dwell on that mentally with faith and all 'walls' of the physical world shall start crumbling to make way just for you and that Promised Land (your ideal) shall then become yours.

"This military strategy which promises victory should not be divulged beforehand."

With this technique, victory is yours! You should always remember to *"pray to your Father… in secret, and your Father… shall reward you openly"* (Matthew 6:6). That is to say, there is no need to be vocal of your desire by struggling to attain it physically. Instead, tune within yourself and meditate on that vision so that it objectifies itself in good time.

So, if you are currently unemployed but you are eyeing on a job, close your eyes and send Rahab to dwell in the 'house' that implies the fulfilment of your desire (that is to be employed). Experience it within as you would experience it without when you are told that the job is already yours. Meditate and mentally 'feel' the employer's handshake congratulating you for your new employment. Also, mentally 'hear' his voice as he congratulates you. 'Feel' the feeling of gratitude for you have just received a new source of income. Repeat these steps over and over again until you come to a state of self-satisfaction that you no longer desire that particular thing because you are convicted in the belief that it is already yours.

夫未戰而廟算勝者，得算多也；未戰而廟算不勝者，得算少也；多算勝，少算不勝，而況於無算乎？吾以此觀之，勝負見矣。

The General who usually wins a battle conducts an assessment extensively in the temple; The General who carries out very shallow assessments is bound to lose the battle.

Therefore, if victory is ensured when extensive assessment is carried out, whereas failure ensues when little assessment is made, imagine how much worse the situation will be without any assessment at all! Hence, by observing these facts, I can already foresee victory or failure.

Temples are sacred places for worship. The true temple lies within you. Again here, the Bible suggests to *"pray behind closed doors"* (Matthew 6:6). This tells you to close the doors of the physical senses and conduct the process of Self-enquiry within instead. The deeper you probe within, the greater clarity you shall gain about your current position in your situation. This will help you decide which line of thoughts to keep and which line of thoughts that should be eliminated to bring you closer to your ideal.

People who do not conduct Self-enquiry do not realise who they really are. They see themselves as mere flesh bound on this physical plane that are meant to succumb to circumstances instead of knowing that they are actually spiritual beings with immense power. Without realising this, their earthly endeavours often end in *failure*. Those who float on the ocean of life without knowing the Self are subjected to the will of others who have recognised the Law. The greater the recognition of one's willpower, the greater the power one possesses. As Thomas Troward says, *"this is the grand natural order of the universe"*.

2 - 作戰

WAGING WAR

孫子曰：凡用兵之法，馳車千駟，革車千乘，帶甲十萬；千里饋糧，則內外之費賓客之用，膠漆之材，車甲之奉，日費千金，然後十萬之師舉矣。

Sun Tzu said: For waging war, we would require one thousand swift horse chariots, one thousand heavy military chariots and one hundred thousand armoured soldiers with enough resources to carry them over a distance of one thousand li. There are also expenses of paying stipends to home and foreign advisors, expenses for materials such as glue and paint and expenses spent for chariots and armour, all of which cost one thousand pieces of gold per day. This is the cost of forming an army of one hundred thousand men.

The importance of thorough preparation cannot be stressed enough to ready oneself for any battle. Sun Tzu emphasises that there must be *enough resources* to transport the army and their necessities over a distance of *one thousand li*. Like any battle, it is not necessarily resolved in a day or two. In life, it is easy to break a pattern but it would take a longer time to form one. Therefore, to prepare for an inner battle to overthrow a habitual pattern that is not beneficial to attain your ideal, you will have to muster all the courage and willpower that you have to survive the journey.

An advisor is defined as one whom you turn to for direction. So, just as *"there are expenses of paying stipends to home and foreign advisors..."*, man not only invests his energy by tuning into his inner Self to shape the ideal, but also in carrying out his daily tasks so as to ensure the successful attainment of it. A strong volition is therefore necessary in forming a solid foundation to prepare for the quest of mastering the mind.

其用戰也貴勝，久則鈍兵挫銳，攻城則力屈，久暴師則國用不足。夫鈍兵，挫銳，屈力，殫貨，則諸侯乘其弊而起，雖有智者，不能善其後矣！故兵聞拙速，未睹巧之久也；夫兵久而國利者，未之有也。

When engaging in battle, if victory is not attained as quickly as possible, the men's weapons will then start to get blunt and their ardour will also be dampened. To then besiege a town, one's strength shall also be exhausted. Therefore, the resources of the State will deplete and will be insufficient for a prolonged battle. Now, when your weapons are dulled, the ardour of the men are dampened and their strength exhausted, and resources depleted, this gives an opportunity to other feudal lords to take advantage of the situation. By then, even the wisest man cannot avert the consequences that must follow. Although one has heard of foolish haste during military operations, skill and intelligence have never been associated with a prolonged battle. Therefore, no State has ever benefited from a prolonged warfare.

The beginning of a quest to work towards a new ideal often shows infinite promises.

It is important not to procrastinate in the effort to attain one's ideal because as time passes, man's energy gets depleted, his hope diminishes, his enthusiasm fails and he will start falling back on the promise he first made to himself.

All these are caused by a weak willpower. Man's willpower fails him because he himself fails his own willpower by not remaining faithful to the ideal he desires. Not being firm with your ideal portrays a possession of weak willpower, which will continue to weaken day by day and this will affect all your future endeavours to achieve anything unless the pattern is broken. Willpower, one's mental strength, is a necessary element in the mastery of the mind. It is therefore crucial to train it so that it will serve you well by giving you the necessary strength to persevere until the realisation of your goal.

A weakened willpower is the trap that causes one's life to be frustrated, miserable and repetitive. This is how the potential of changing one's life is often whittled away, also leading to low morale. When this happens, man becomes a victim to other negative thought patterns that cause his life to spiral down further.

Even those who know of the Universal Law, however wise, *cannot avert the consequences that must follow* from nurturing a weak willpower.

Therefore, when you have decided to attain a particular goal, dedicate yourself (both in thought and physical effort) to work towards it unceasingly. Rid yourself immediately of all that do not promote the realisation of that goal and instead, adopt all that do. Nip them in the bud this instant so that they do not continue to grow within you. Do all that are necessary until that ideal objectifies itself on the physical plane. Procrastination only brings more harm than good.

故不盡知用兵之害者，則不能盡知用兵之利也。善用兵者，役不再籍，糧不三載，取用于國，因糧于敵，故軍食可足也。

One who is not well versed with the troubles of warfare cannot possibly know its rewards. A skilled army does not raise troops twice or transport its supplies three times and brings equipment from home. Such army relies on provisions from the enemy. In this way, resources will definitely be sufficient to maintain the army.

One who is not familiar with the mischievous nature of the mind will not know the art and reward of mastering it. You must have a master plan for everything that you do. When Sun Tzu mentions that *"a skilled army does not raise troops twice or transport its supplies three times"*, he is referring to the practice of foresight to minimise unnecessary wastage of resources (in Mental Science: energy and individual volition). You will need to be able to draw a plan consisting of the steps necessary in bringing your goal or ideal to completion.

When you have set yourself a new year's resolution, plan wisely the steps to be taken in bringing your resolution into reality. It is foolish for one to make a resolution without any concrete plan. It leads you to not take it seriously and abandoning it halfway through only to make that same resolution again the next year. This again highlights the utilisation of weak willpower.

It is similar to driving a car. Your foot has to be on the accelerator pedal all the time. When you remove your foot, friction takes over and the car slows down. Even if you were to put your foot back onto the pedal again, it will take some time before the same momentum is built. It is not only a waste of energy but also time.

Therefore, have a clear mental picture of your ideal and step on the accelerator of your mind to work towards it. All the tasks that have to be done have to be completed now. Be assured that today's work that is completed today is a promise for tomorrow, whereas today's work that is not done today is a failure for tomorrow.

To change his circumstances, the wise Commander turns to the Self by using his mind to visualise the exact ideal he would like to see objectify in his surroundings. He then walks on this physical plane as though his ideal is true. Neville Goddard once said that *"an assumption though false, if persisted in will harden into fact"*. Man's *enemy*, the current reality on the physical plane that defies the experience of his ideal will begin to change to conform to the image he has conjured in his mind. Opportunities, *provisions* that you can *rely on*, will present themselves out of the blue to help bring your ideal into reality. You may then be required to take 'inspired action'.

國之貧于師者遠輸，遠輸則百姓貧，近于師者貴賣，貴賣則百姓財竭，財竭則急于丘役，力屈財殫，中原內虛于家，百姓之費，十去其七，公家之費，破車罷馬，甲冑矢弩，戟楯蔽櫓，丘牛大車，十去其六。

The State will be impoverished if the army has to be maintained from a distance. On the other hand, the prices of goods escalate high in places that are in proximity of an army, causing drainage to the citizens' wealth. To cope with the expenses, the peasants will also be afflicted with higher taxation. Because of this, people will lose their homes, 70% of their income will be dissipated; and the government's expenses for war material such as damaged chariots, worn-out horses, armour, helmets, arrows, spears, shields and wagons will also amount to 60% of its total reserve.

When man 'sees' his ideal as being far from him instead of as already possessing it, it drains him of his energy, hope and enthusiasm to work towards it. By remaining ignorant to the Law, man is deprived of living life to its fullest potential.

On the other hand, in his endless external pursuit of material comforts, man is also vulnerable to the decline of actual wealth - one's internal values. Man today is capable of going to any extent to attain his desire even if it means defying his personality and principles and causing harm to another being. The sacrifice that comes along with ignorance is too great and unnecessary.

There really is no need to deprive others of anything at all in order to objectify your goal in your current reality. So long one applies the Universal Law in one's life, everything will fall into place harmoniously by itself.

故智將務食于敵，食敵一鍾，當吾二十鍾，萁稈一石，當我廿石。故殺敵者怒也，取敵之利者貨也。故車戰，得車十乘以上，賞其先得者，而更其旌旗，車雜而乘之，卒善而養之，是謂勝敵而益強。

Hence, a wise General will seek to use his enemy to maintain his own army. A portion of the enemy's provision is equivalent to twenty of one's own and one picul of fodder is similarly equivalent to twenty of one's own. The soldiers require rage to kill the enemy. So, they may be motivated by the advantages of seizing the enemy's good as a reward. When ten or more chariots are seized during a chariot-fight, reward the one who had captured the first one. Then, substitute the enemy's flags with one's own. The chariots from the enemy should be mixed and used in conjunction with one's own. Captives should be kept and treated with kindness. This is what we call by using the enemy to augment one's own strength.

Hence, the wise man will construct the image of his ideal within and let the world that surrounds him be transformed to present opportunities at his doorstep to bring his ideal into reality. This is the most effective method to change reality than one's endless frantic physical pursuit of it.

A strong volition is necessary before any transformation of the surrounding reality can actually take place. Determine the basis of your ideal. For example, the creation of a mattress started with the desire for a more comfortable sleep. With this came into the mind of the inventor a mental image of a soft bed. The same principle applies to every single material object or goal that you are in pursuit of. The great railway magnate James J. Hill was *motivated* to provide a service for people to travel from coast to coast. Before this became a fact in his current reality, Hill 'travelled' the tracks daily in his mind until the tracks were finally laid.

Therefore, find that basis of your ideal whatever it may be and remain fixated on the vision until a strong volition is formed. That is the fuel by which you will travel with to attain your ideal. Be assured that in time, your current experience of reality will make way for your mental picture to materialise.

Even amidst adversity, turn it into a benefit. The terrain that your 'enemy' once owned will then become yours as you *substitute his flags* with your own. However, remember that ego should never be at play even after you have successfully realised your goals. Just as Sun Tzu says, "*captives should be kept and treated with kindness*". The fact that you have successfully re-written your seeming previous fate and materialised your ideal is due to the Universal Law. Thomas Troward cautions to treat this fact as a perfectly natural result, which had been reached through one's demand from the infinite supply (the Self). Remaining steadfast to the Law (the Cause) without one's attention being distracted with the outcome of his circumstances (the resulting factor), man's faith in the Self and inner strength are deepened further.

故兵貴勝，不貴久；故知兵之將，民之司命，國家安危之主也。

Therefore, let victory, instead of prolonged battle, be the goal. A General who is well-versed with military related factors is verily the determinant of the fate of both the citizens and the State.

Therefore, give unwavering attention to your ideal and do not let anything distract your attention. Buddha said that you are the result of your thoughts. So, manage them properly and you will determine the outcome of your life, which will also affect the rest of the people who surround you.

3 - 謀攻

STRATEGY OF ATTACK

孫子曰：凡用兵之法，全國為上，破國次之；全旅為上，破旅次之；全卒為上，破卒次之；全伍為上，破伍次之。

Sun Tzu said: Taking an enemy's country intact is better than having a shattered one, possessing a whole troop is better than a shattered one, maintaining a whole army of soldiers is better than destroying them, and keeping the whole squad is better than losing them.

Here, Sun Tzu implies that there is no need for the exertion of external negative forces to change reality. When you look into the mirror and you do not like what you see, change the

41

face but not break the mirror. Not only does it not change a thing by breaking the mirror, you may also end up hurting yourself!

Unite with the forces of nature and be guided from the Source within you. When you do the things that do not resonate with your inner feelings, you are resisting the flow. Flowing with the current of the inner river of infinite intelligence to objectify your ideals is better than fighting against it.

To attain their objectives, many resort to unrighteous practices such as cheating, lying and fighting as they do not realise that they possess this infinite power within them, which requires no force whatsoever on the outside to shape an end. Oscar Wilde says to *"believe in yourself and there will come a day when others will have no choice but to believe with you."* When you rely on the Universal Law to objectify your goals into reality, everything will start falling into place harmoniously and with the right mental attitude, you may even end up having more than what you had initially bargained for.

是故百戰百勝，非善之善者也；不戰而屈人之兵，善之善者也。

Therefore, to successfully secure victory for one hundred battles does not denote supreme excellence but to subdue the enemy's resistance without fighting, is.

Therefore, it is not so significant how many times you have successfully changed your circumstances to attain your ideal but *how* you do it is most important.

To be able to manipulate an adverse situation and steer your mind to focus on the ideal that you would like objectified in your reality denotes excellence. You should develop unwavering faith in the Self by which all worldly experiences are rooted in. The Universal Law shall then help you break any resisting patterns without as soon as you have changed your thinking pattern within. That is how you *subdue* your *enemy's resistance* without fighting.

故上兵伐謀，其次伐交，其次伐兵，其下攻城。攻城之法，為不得已；修櫓轒轀，具器械，三月而後成；距闉，又三月而後已；將不勝其忿，而蟻附之，殺士卒三分之一，而城不拔者，此攻之災也。

The best strategy of warfare is therefore to first try to disrupt the enemy's plan. The next best strategy would be cutting off their alliances. Third best is to attack the enemy's army. The last resort is to launch an attack on walled cities. Only when no other options are available should one resort to this decision.

Preparing turrets (portable watch tower), war chariots and other weapons will require at least three months. After that, piling up mounds against the walls will also take another three months more.

The General who is unable to contain his anger will send his soldiers swarming the walls like ants, resulting in one-third of them being killed while the city still remains unconquered. Such is the price of the attempt of attacking a walled city.

Although the reality of your life appears to be absolute, it is in fact not so. At the moment, it may seem to be heading towards a certain direction, which you cannot escape. However, you can *disrupt* the *plan* by turning within your Self and change your beliefs and concepts of your current situation. The Law then cannot fail you for as within, so without.

Negative emotions and negative thoughts are your biggest enemies. Before they begin to govern your life, nip them in the bud.

If you are unable to gain complete mastery of your mind in being selective of the thoughts you choose to contemplate on, cut the cord with naysayers and remove everything in your immediate environment that suggests otherwise so that your focus on your ideal is not distracted. Why keep them when they are feeding your anxiety and doubts?

Most people fall into Sun Tzu's third category, which is to *attack the enemy's army*. They constantly react to circumstances and criticisms, believing that it is necessary to fight against them in order to be 'successful'. They fail to realise that they hold within them a power so great that can move mountains.

Attacking walled cities can be likened to banging one's own head against the wall. Too often man tries to change his external experiences without realising that the actual root lies within.

After experiencing repeated 'failures' in attaining his ideals, man starts to lose his mind and out of desperation, tries to bulldoze his way through. He does whatever it takes without to attain the end he desires. This is dangerous for he becomes vulnerable to the six vices of lust, anger, greed, attachment, pride and hatred. All rationality is then lost when it comes to dealing with his current circumstances. At this stage, he has all to lose but nothing to gain. He cannot keep what is not rightfully his for he has not appropriated his ideal within his own mind. And so, the *city* which he desires *still remains unconquered.*

That is the price man has to pay in attempting to change his worldly experiences by external efforts without changing his thoughts and beliefs within. Too much energy and precious time are lost in such a futile endeavour.

故善用兵者，屈人之兵，而非戰也；拔人之城，而非攻也；毀人之國，而非久也。必以全爭于天下，故兵不頓，利可全，此謀攻之法也。

Therefore, a skilful leader in military operations is able to subdue the enemy's resistance without fighting, conquer a kingdom without attacking and overthrow the enemy without prolonged battle. His aim is to take everything 'under the heaven' intact. This is the military strategy that helps procure the enemy's nation, yet prevents the forces from being worn out.

You now know that the best way to change your circumstances is to change your beliefs within. Doing so will enable man to *subdue* external forces *without fighting*. The wise one realises that there is no need to harm himself or others in order to appropriate his ideal. So long he remains faithful to his mental image, everything will start falling into place harmoniously. The one who is a Master of his mind will never allow the seeds of doubt, anxiety and fear to grow within him. He uproots them immediately whenever they arise. Then, it will not be long before his ideal objictifies in his current physical reality.

This is how man takes everything *'under the heaven' intact* without having to experience huge losses.

Therefore, send *Rahab* (which is your imagination as explained in Chapter 1) to *procure* your desired city (your ideal). As you direct *Rahab* to occupy a specific state, you are appropriating the ideal within you. The walls of the walled city must then crumble effortlessly just as it was written in scripture to make way for you to objectify the ideal.

故用兵之法，十則圍之，五則攻之，倍則分之，敵則能戰之，少則能守之，不若則能避之。故小敵之堅，大敵之擒也。

The rule in military operation is to surround the enemy when our force is ten to one, to attack them when it is five to one, to divide the army when our force is two to one, and to battle with them if both forces are matched. If however our force is fewer than the enemy's, defend against them. Avoid the enemy altogether if our strength does not match theirs. One who is still determined to pursue battle despite having a weak force is bound to lose to the enemy.

Sun Tzu emphasises on the importance of analysing one's own state of mind and position. You must be able to evaluate your own strengths and weaknesses, and act upon them accordingly.

Without correcting the mind and strengthening the will, your attempt to fight and change external circumstances will be to no avail. Over time, your energy gets depleted and your persistence and enthusiasm will decrease. Out of desperation, you will then begin to doubt your own ability and inner power. Finally, you end up surrendering to your *enemy*, your doubts, without realising your goal.

夫將者，國之輔也，輔周則國必強，輔隙則國必弱。

The General is the one responsible for the State's security. If total safety measures are adopted, the State is strong. If however the measures are flawed, the State will be weak.

Destiny is dependent on oneself. The *safety measures* to be adopted are to safeguard the mind from the invasion of non-constructive thought patterns, feelings and emotions to give way for desirable seeds (good thoughts or intention) to grow so that they become strongly rooted in one's mind.

If your *measures* of protecting the mind from the invasion of doubts, fear and anxiety are *flawed*, your overall well-being and goal are at stake. The mind becomes weak and your destiny appears unclear. Therefore, always be alert and remove all the weeds from this divine garden of your mind as they come to your attention.

故軍之所以患于君者三：不知三軍之不可以進，而謂之進；不知三軍之不可以退，而謂之退；是謂縻軍。不知三軍之事，而同三軍之政，則軍士惑矣。不知三軍之權，而同三軍之任，則軍士疑矣。三軍既惑且疑，則諸侯之難至矣，是謂亂軍引勝。

There are three ways by which the Ruler can pose difficulty to the army:

1) *By commanding the army to advance when it cannot do so, or ordering a retreat when the army is in no position to withdraw. This is known as meddling with army matters;*

2) *By governing the army in the same manner as he rules the kingdom whilst remaining ignorant of army-related affairs. This will confuse the officers and soldiers; and*

3) *By appointing officers to come into power without proper discrimination and ignorance of military rules will shake the confidence of the army.*

When the army is confused and in doubt, other feudal lords will take the advantage of stirring more trouble. Such chaos will only lead to the enemy's victory.

Although resources are available for one to utilise to bring dreams into reality, one may obstruct the natural workings of the Law to objectify an ideal in various ways.

1) It is impossible to force an ideal to come into being and eradicate undesirable circumstances without correcting the state of the mind; for example, the Law simply cannot grant one riches when one's mind still dwells on thoughts of poverty.

2) Being ignorant of the Law and the nature of the mind is the key factor in impeding the objectification of one's goal. Merely recognising that the Law exists is not enough. You must practice it. It is sheer hypocrisy to acknowledge the existence of such great power and yet not use it. Foolish are those who say that they are infinite beings of limitless possibilities but still choose to subject themselves to their circumstances. It is important for one to practice the unity of thoughts, words and actions for their integration denotes purity. When your words, thoughts and actions are not in harmony with each other, there is bound to be inner clashes that cause restlessness and confusion.

3) Allowing circumstances and other people to have power over you can be destructive to your self-*confidence* and willpower. Over time, you may develop the habit of submitting yourself to what the five external senses perceive instead of relying on the Self in your journey to objectify your ideals.

In ancient China, the Ruler was the one with immeasurable power by which everyone swore allegiance to. Many spiritual scriptures and even modern quantum physics seem to point out that a universe cannot exist without the mind.

Although the mind is responsible for the outward manifestation of the entire universe and your circumstances, it is a folly to let it run free according to its whim and fancy. The play of the mind in causing misery is cyclical and will not end unless the cycle is broken. The mind has the power to project itself to take the form of an ideal and yet so easily become the victim to its very own creation, forgetting that it was the one responsible for it.

For example, one who dwells on images of poverty in his mind can only experience poverty in his surrounding reality. This experience of poverty then tricks the mind, which has forgotten that it was the causing factor in the first place, to again dwell on the similar plane of thoughts and hence re-creating the same experience. The experience cannot change until the cycle is broken; that is to exercise a change in the pattern of one's thoughts.

Therefore, discipline the mind by employing the Intellect to discriminate the ideals that are worthy of your contemplation for them to objectify in your current reality.

故知勝者有五：知可以戰與不可以戰者勝，識眾寡之用者勝，上下同欲者勝，以虞待不虞者勝，將能而君不御者勝；此五者，知勝之道也。

And so there are five factors to secure victory:

1) *He who knows when is the right moment to fight or not to fight will be victorious;*
2) *He who knows how to handle both big and small forces of the army will be victorious;*
3) *He who knows how to unite the entire army, both of superior and inferior ranks alike with the same spirit of attaining a common goal will be victorious;*
4) *He who has prepared himself but waits for the right moment to overthrow the enemy who is unprepared will be victorious; and,*
5) *He who is capable in military affairs without the Ruler interfering in the operations will be victorious.*

These are the five factors outlining one's victory.

Sun Tzu prescribes five factors of which one must adhere to secure victory:

1) It is important for one to know when exactly the right moment is to take action. As soon as you start picturing an ideal in your mind, many opportunities will start coming your way. This is the Universal Law in play, showing you that you are on the right track as you progress towards your ideal. When this happens, remember to never settle for anything less than what you truly want.

   For example, I knew someone who wanted a high-definition television in his room. However, he was not willing to part with his money to purchase it. I told him to drop his intent on the Universal Mind that he had received his high-definition television for free. He was to imagine to his very best the physical features and specifications of the television as vividly as he could in his mind.

Since then, he started attracting to his experience various advertisements on discounted deals for that item, information on monthly-repayment plans and more. Some deals were very attractive and he could see no other way to get that television but to pay for it. I reminded him that since he had invoked the power within him to materialise the television set for free, his ideal must come to pass. Neville Goddard once said that an assumption, though false, when persisted in will harden into fact.

With that, he refrained from taking action until few days later when his sister suddenly gave him hers as she had to suddenly move to another house and there was no place to put the television in her new room. This time, he took action; he accepted the set. The television he received had the exact specifications as what he had wanted in his mind.

2) Sun Tzu suggests that flexibility plays an important role in ensuring success. Regardless of how little your immediate physical resources are, one who can still manage and utilise them effectively is bound to succeed. The resources that we can perceive with our five senses are not as important as utilising the inner senses and the power of the mind to objectify our ideals.

3) You must know how to unite your forces to direct them towards a specific objective. One must sacrifice the concept of the present self that you are not happy with to assume the new state that you desire. The Self,

intellect, mind and senses must be united in order for man to practice one-pointedness to attain his goals. Only with this can one be victorious in objectifying an ideal.

4) The *enemy* in Sun Tzu's context refers to the current reality that seems absolute; an unchangeable fate. Because the world of matter (duality) exists with the illusion of 'ego', the external senses have a tendency to conclude any current experience of reality as a final fact. The one born from above (one who realises the power of the Self) however, will know how to overcome any undesirable circumstances. All that one has to do is to replace the memory of one's current experience with the vision of a desirable ideal in the mind and wait for it to materialise on the objective plane. By doing so, you would have then *overthrown the enemy* (the ego experience) *who was unprepared* since the mind has previously been conditioned to accept all outer experiences as being true and unalterable.

5) It is extremely important for one to know the nature of the mind and how it works before one can successfully apply the principles to lead the life of one's ideal. When you know how the nature of the Universal Mind, you are liberated from life's limiting circumstances.

"Mind is the cause of bondage or liberation. Mind absorbed in sense objects is the cause of bondage, and mind detached from the sense objects is the cause of liberation." (Amrta-bindu Upanisad 2).

Once you recognise and appreciate the nature of the mind, you can avoid obstructing the natural workings of the Law to objectify any of your ideal in life and instead, use it to attain the highest purpose of your existence.

故曰：知彼知己，百戰不殆；不知彼而知己，一勝一負；不知彼，不知己，每戰必敗。

Therefore, it is said that: one who knows the enemy and himself need not fear the danger of one hundred battles. On the other hand, one who knows himself, but not the enemy, has an equal chance of either winning or losing. Worse still, one who does not know himself and the enemy is vulnerable to danger in every battle.

For those who *know* the true nature of the Self and the nature of the *'enemy'* (the illusion conjured by the mind) *need not fear the danger* of falling prey to undesirable circumstances. Those who however only recognise the existence of the supremacy of the Self but do not understand the nature of the mind may sometimes be successful in objectifying his or her ideals, but may also sometimes experience failed attempts.

The worst category that one can fall into is that of not knowing both the power of the Self and the illusion conjured by the mind. Those falling into this category are *vulnerable to the danger* of losing every *battle* in life as they waddle through the uncertainties that surround them.

4 - 軍形

FORMATION OF ARMY

孫子曰：昔之善戰者，先為不可勝，以待敵之可勝，不可勝在己，可勝在敵。故善戰者，能為不可勝，不能使敵必可勝。故曰：勝可知，而不可為。

Sun Tzu said: Great warriors of ancient times first ensured that they were invincible as they waited for the enemy to become vulnerable. Being invincible to secure ourselves from the enemy would depend on oneself, but the opportunity of defeating the enemy is provided by the enemy himself. Therefore, a great warrior may be able to secure himself against defeat by making himself invincible but cannot make the enemy vulnerable. That is why it is said that although one may know how to conquer, it is not necessary that one can do so.

Whatsoever battle you may be fighting for in life, it is important to stay strong and grounded in principles and faith. Such strong grounding will make you *invincible* against the *enemy* of doubt, fear and anxiety. Sun Tzu suggests that the strength to become *invincible* is dependent upon oneself. The more *invincible* one's mind is, the less likely one will be defeated by the inner devil of doubt. Being convicted in one's ideal can safeguard one's vision from being swayed by the uncertainty of circumstances.

So, train your mind that it accepts no external suggestions from circumstances that will lead it to start doubting its capability of attaining an ideal except that that emanates from the Self.

The man who stands strongly on his ground and has faith in his ideal need not fear while he patiently *waits for the enemy to become vulnerable*. As the saying goes, "Truth always prevails." Just as a ray of light chases away darkness, so does the Light of faith *conquer* the inner devil of doubt, fear and anxiety. As you persevere in your goal through exercising the power of right thought, the strength of your enemy is bound to weaken as time passes by.

Therefore, shape your mind to become *invincible* to *secure yourself against defeat* by the inner devil. Bear in mind however that Sun Tzu believes that building yourself to be invincible *does not make the enemy vulnerable*. Although invincibility strengthens your willpower to objectify an ideal, unless the elements of doubt, fear and anxiety (the *enemy*) are eradicated from one's consciousness, the promised land (ideal) can never be *conquered* (materialise).

That is why it is said that although one may know how to conquer (to objectify one's ideal), *it is not necessary that one can do so*. Mere knowledge is not sufficient. It is important to apply that knowledge into action.

不可勝者，守也；可勝者，攻也。守則不足，攻則有餘。善守者，藏于九地之下；善攻者，動于九天之上，故能自保而全勝也。

The one who is not certain of victory relies on invincibility to defend against defeat. But one who is certain of victory attacks the enemy. It is not enough to merely defend oneself. Attacking, which exemplifies superior strength, is also necessary. Excelling in defence conceals oneself in the deepest depths of the Earth, whereas excelling in attack advances oneself beyond the nine Heavens. Therefore, one who is skilled in both tactics can protect oneself against the enemy and also secure complete victory.

Not convinced of the Universal Law, one still gives room for doubt, fear and anxiety (the enemy) to lurk in the mind. Therefore, one *relies* on the *invincibility* of the mind *to defend against defeat*. This often happens when you are not convicted in the belief that your ideal will materialise in your experience.

In attempting to train your mind to conform to the ideals you have at heart, one is inclined to constantly feed the mind with positive suggestions to counter the negative ones. The knowledge of the Law of Mental Science motivates one to *defend* oneself against negative suggestions, but it is *not enough*. When there is still a need to defend oneself from the doubting Thomas within you, it simply means that you are still operating on the basis of doubt instead of faith.

As mentioned in the above, the Promised Land (ideal) cannot be conquered unless the enemy is completely eradicated from the mind.

Chinese mythology and folklore often narrate of the existence of a mythological creature called a dragon. The dragon is the most ancient emblem of supreme spiritual power, wisdom and strength. It is believed that they inhabit the *deepest depths* of the watery region of *the Earth*. The dragon is likened to the dormant power and brilliance of the Self, which await to be uncovered *from the depth of the Earth* (circumstances) so that it may *advance beyond the nine Heavens* to where it rightfully belongs. This signifies the awakening of man so that he may use the inner power latent within him to rise above circumstances and be the Master of himself.

Therefore, possessing both an *invincible* mind and the skill to *attack* the enemy is necessary in one's journey towards mastering the mind. As the enemy of doubt arises, the man with an *invincible* mind protects himself by reaffirming that what he seeks already exists within the Self and will objectify in good time. When paired with the *skill* to eradicate the enemy, one can then swiftly uproot the negative thoughts and emotions to prevent them from branching out further. With that, one can then *secure complete victory*.

見勝，不過眾人之所知，非善之善者也。戰勝，而天下曰善，非善之善者也。故舉秋毫，不為多力；見日月，不為明目；聞雷霆，不為聰耳。

Victory, as how most people define it to be, does not denote the quality of excellence. Even when the whole world applauds and praises the victory of a battle, the victory still need not necessarily have been borne out of excellence. As we all know, to lift a fine feather does not imply great strength, to see the sun and moon does not indicate one possesses sharp vision and neither is one considered to have a quick ear for hearing the sound of thunder.

Most people believe that the mere attainment of a certain end that they desire implies *victory*. Not knowing the

Universal Law, one has a tendency to exert too much pressure or force, with some resorting to unscrupulous means to attain an end result. These are the people who dwell on the thought-frequency of lack for they do not know the Law of Abundance.

Even if *the whole world* believes and *applauds* you for the work that you do or the *victory* that you have secured, it may not have been *borne out of excellence*. Therefore, do not follow the herd but instead, aim to expand your mind. An achievement that can be perceived and accepted as being possible by so many does not distinguish you from the rest. Just as Sun Tzu says, to be able to *lift a fine feather* (overcome a light challenge) does not show one's *strength*, to be able to *see* what everyone else sees does not indicate that one possesses a *sharp vision*, and to *hear* what others can hear does not imply that one has a *quick ear*.

A Master is one who has mastered the art of mind over matter. Therefore, the Master is one who has the courage and is prepared to take on the challenge of materialising an ideal that others deem impossible to attain. Also possessing a trained inner vision, the Master is one who has perfected the art of seeing the invisible; the reality that is yet to objectify itself on this third-dimensional plane. The man who is the Master of his mind is also able to experience the reality of his ideal with the five inner senses as if they were already true in this objective world. That is indeed the hallmark of real *victory*.

古之善戰者，勝于易勝者；故善戰者之勝也，無智名，無勇功。故其戰勝不忒，不忒者，其措必勝，勝已敗者也。故善戰者，立于不敗之地，而不失敵之敗也。是故勝兵先勝，而後求戰；敗兵先戰，而後求勝。

Ancient good warriors are not those who win battles, but those who win them with ease; great warriors do not owe their victory to their fame for wisdom nor accomplishment of bravery. They win their battles when they give no room for mistakes. Victory is certain for those who do not commit mistakes as one conquers the enemy that has already been defeated. Therefore, great warriors always ensure that they remain in a position that they cannot be defeated as well as not missing any opportunity of overthrowing the enemy. The army that secures victory first and only then seeks battle will be victorious. Those who attempt to fight first however, and then only seek victory are doomed for defeat.

Sun Tzu believes that *good warriors* of any battle are not those who win them, but those who have perfected the art to *win them with ease*. It is neither the *wisdom* nor *courage* that one musters within to put the Law to the test in objectifying an ideal that leads one to victory. Instead, to obtain victory in the mastery of the mind, one cannot commit mistakes. A mistake is committed when one, by the act of doubt, puts a limit on the infinite power that verily created the Universe. The Bible states that "*unless you believe that I am He, you will die in your sins.*" (John 8:24). So, unless you realise the nature of the Self, you are sinning because the Self is the embodiment of limitless possibilities.

A great warrior is one who gives no room for negative thoughts and feelings to sprout within his mind. Therefore, *commit no mistakes* and nip the inner devil of doubt before it becomes strongly enrooted in your mind. Be faithful to the Universal Law and know that to the Self, no ideal is ever too great for it to objectify. Remember your place as the child of Truth and Light. Since *"Man is made in the image of God"* (Genesis 1:26), there can be nothing that is impossible unto you. Just as Genevieve Behrend says, *"nothing can prevent your picture from coming into concrete form except the same power which gave it birth - yourself."*

With such conviction in the Law, *never miss an opportunity* to eradicate the enemy from the divine garden of your mind whenever they come to your attention. If you allow negative thoughts and feelings to breed within you, it is similar to allowing weeds to grow in your garden. Slowly, these weeds will cause your plants (ideals) to die, one by one.

Therefore, to *ascertain victory*, envision your ideal vividly in your mind and eliminate all doubts that you are separated from that ideal. In this way, you are bound to be victorious. Those who waddle through life fighting circumstances with no specific goal(s) are fighting a futile battle; one that they are *doomed for defeat*.

善用兵者，修道而保法，故能為勝敗之政。兵法：「一曰度，二曰量，三曰數，四曰稱，五曰勝；地生度，度生量，量生數，數生稱，稱生勝。」故勝兵若以鎰稱銖，敗兵若以銖稱鎰。勝者之戰，若決積水于千仞之谿，形也。

Good soldiers cultivate the Path and preserve the Rule. They can therefore govern victory or defeat. The strategies employed in military affairs are:

1)   *To Estimate*
2)   *To Measure*

3)   To Calculate
4)   To Weigh
5)   Victory

Estimation is made possible based on the Earth factor; measurement is derived from estimation, calculations from measurement, comparisons from calculations, and victory from comparisons. Therefore, a victorious army will be likened to a pound measured against a single grain, whereas a defeated army will be perceived as a single grain weighed against a pound. A victorious army possesses a force, which form is likened to the bursting of amassed water into a gorge that is one thousand ren deep.

The awakened man is one who sets *the Path* by familiarising himself with the Universal Law (refer to Chapter 1) and operates his life with it. The decision to make an ideal alive or dead rests upon him. He also adheres strictly to *the Rule*, which is the hierarchy of governing faculties within himself; namely the Soul, intellect, mind and the senses. The awakened one recognises the Soul as the Master of the intellect, the intellect as the Master of the mind, and the mind as the Master of the senses. Equipped with the wisdom of the Soul, man can then draw *the Path* by directing the intellect to guide the mind, which in turn controls his senses to dwell only on factors that bring his ideals to fruition. With that, he has the power to change his circumstances and ultimately, his destiny.

There are three stages that one must go through to secure victory in manifesting their ideal. They are *concentration*, *contemplation* and *meditation*. These three stages are implemented in the step step-by-step *strategy* found below:

1) To Estimate

You must initiate an ideal. Know exactly what you want to objectify in your experience. Remember that you are dealing with a potential energy that is yet to be differentiated into a particular form. Therefore, differentiate it into any specific form that you will. *Concentrate* within and you will discover exactly what you would like to manifest in your life experience.

2) To Measure

Once you have an idea of what you would like to materialise, *contemplate* and give the ideal some depth. For example, if wanting a new house is your ideal, then specifically define its characteristics in your mind. Mentally walk through that house and note the size and shape of the house, the number of rooms it has and where you would place each furniture piece.

If money is what you want to objectify in your experience, then define exactly how much of it that you require. As you define the specifics of the ideal in your mind, you are already constructing the structure of the object in the fourth-dimensional plane, which will materialise itself in this objective world in good time.

3) To Calculate

Now that you have a vivid image of the ideal that you want to objectify in your experience, it is time to analyse your state of mind. List down the basis of the motivation behind your ideal. For example, the basis of motivation behind wanting a car is to have the convenience of transport and the motivation behind owning a house is the feeling of security.

However, be very careful when you attempt to define the ultimate end result that you would like to experience in your life. Remember to always see the larger picture. For example, one who would like to master the skill of typing may not want it solely for the sake of possessing the skill itself but instead, aims to use it for other motives. Perhaps the person would like to master the skill of typing so that he or she can be promoted to the next level at their workplace? When you analyse the motivation further, you may discover that the desire to be promoted is actually to have a salary increase. If an increase in salary is really what you want, dwell on that instead of focusing your attention to master the skill of typing. The increase of salary can come to you in many other ways. Therefore, the result of such analysis will reveal to you the real motivation behind the definition of an ideal.

Whatever it may be, dwell on the ideal until a strong volition is developed within you. As mentioned in Chapter 2, a strong volition is necessary to keep you on track to attain a goal.

Then, conduct a mental assessment by analysing the reasons as to why you believe you are worthy of that ideal and why you think you are not. A clear and honest review will help you identify your thoughts and categorise them as being either 'friends' or 'foe'.

4) To Weigh

After all the *calculations*, *weigh* your factors. Are there any negative thoughts and feelings related to the externalisation of your ideal? If negative thoughts do exist within you, do your positive thoughts outweigh the negative ones? Do your best to counter each negative point with a positive affirmation. An example is shown below:

Goal: *To buy a new house.*

Why I cannot...	Why I can...
Insufficient funds.	Money is like everything else in the Universe. It is just an idea. All exist within me. So, if I tune my awareness to money, the Law must manifest it in my experience.

5) *Victory*

Having concentrated and contemplated on your ideal, you must now meditate on it. With meditation, everything is possible. Most spiritual teachers believe that the experiences in life are determined by the ideas imprinted on the subconscious mind.

As the mind becomes still during meditation, a bridge is formed between the conscious mind and the subconscious mind. One is then able to direct his or her conscious mind to impregnate the subconscious mind with an ideal, which will materialise in one's objective reality over time.

Therefore, visualise your ideal vividly in your mind's eye without any trace of doubt and you can be sure that victory is already yours. The man who is victorious in mastering his mind will allow no obstacles to stop him from objectifying his ideal. His journey through life will be one that is full of force and vigour. Sun Tzu's metaphor of *amassed water bursting into a gorge that is one thousand ren deep* depicts the image of a man who possesses a strong willpower with an unstoppable mission.

5 - 兵勢
POTENTIAL

孫子曰：凡治眾如治寡，分數是也。鬥眾如鬥寡，形名是也。三軍之眾，可使必受敵而無敗者，奇正是也。兵之所加，如以碬投卵者，虛實是也。

Sun Tzu said: To manage a large force of army is actually the same with managing a force of few men; both still require dividing the army into smaller units. Similarly, fighting against an enemy who has a large force is also the same with fighting against one who has a small force; both still require fighting the enemy, which is a force of another form with another name. Regardless of the resources and situation, all the three ranks of the army must apply direct and indirect measures in all battles in order to withstand the enemy's attack without being defeated. Raising an army for a battle is dependent on the evaluation of the real situation so that one's military force will create a strong impact that is likened to a solid rock, which is casted on a fragile egg.

Regardless of how big or small your dreams are, the Law works the same way to draw them into your current reality. So, dream as big as you can to your heart's content as no dreamer is ever too small and no dream is ever too big. Famous painter Michelangelo Buonarrati says that *"the danger for most of us lies not in setting our aim too high and falling short, but in setting our aim too low, and achieving our mark"*. Remember that within you lies a power so great that can even move mountains. All you need is to *"take the first step with faith… (even if you cannot) see the whole staircase"* (Martin Luther King, Jr.).

For some, having a big dream can be intimidating for they cannot see how their ideal will materialise itself. It is not important if you do not have any resources that you require to achieve your dreams. Solely by the power of imagination, if you can clearly see and feel the ideal in your mind's eye, the way shall reveal itself to you as nature abhors a vacuum.

Remember that every great structure that was ever built started with a single brick. Therefore, set yourself the ideal that is worthy of you and experience it in your mind as though you are already experiencing it in the flesh. Then, with such conviction, do all the things that will help you shape your dream into reality. If you have set yourself a big goal, break it down into more manageable fragments. This is known as goal-setting. It will help you draw an effective action plan to work towards it.

Like in all journeys, you may face obstacles when trying to objectify your ideal. These obstacles may come in any form be it physical limitations or even opposing ideas from others.

Whatever they may be, remember that these obstacles are also mere concepts, which are simply of *another form* that do not flow in the same direction as yours.

Even if the whole world does not believe in the possibility of the externalisation of your ideal does not mean that your dream is impossible to attain. Just like how an idea that you accept to be true in your mind shapes your reality, the ideas they hold to be true in their minds also shape their destiny. Henry Ford says that *"whether (one) thinks (one) can or cannot, either way (they) are right"*.

Regardless of the amount of *resources* that you have or the *situation* that you face when materialising your ideal, Sun Tzu suggests that it is not enough to just exert physical strength in taking action *(direct measure)*. It is very important that one, who wants to fulfil a desire, to first be familiar with the Universal Law and the nature of the mind. Equipped with such knowledge, man will not easily fall prey to the enemy of doubt, fear and anxiety as he waits for his ideal to materialise on this third-dimensional plane.

Neville Goddard advises one *"to walk by faith and not by sight"*. All that is required of you to objectify your ideal is to have unwavering faith. Be sure to know exactly what your heart truly desires and then weigh carefully as to what further results that the manifestation of your desire will lead to. This *self-evaluation* will help you preserve the momentum necessary to actualise that ideal because one will possess a stronger willpower in working towards an ideal that resonates with one's heart than working towards an ideal that does not. Then, live in the feeling of the wish fulfilled and shut your senses to all that deny you of it.

Man's faith in the Self has a great impact on the way he moves the universal creative force to shape his experiences. The momentum he will then possess to re-arrange circumstances so as to bring his ideal into being is likened to *"a solid rock that is casted on a fragile egg"*.

凡戰者，以正合，以奇勝。故善出奇者，無窮如天地，不竭如江河，終而復始，日月是也；死而復生，四時是也。

In all battles, direct measures are used to fight, but the employment of indirect measures is necessary to secure victory. Therefore, those who are skilled at employing indirect measures in battles will never be impoverished just like Heaven and Earth, never exhausted like the flow of the Great rivers, and like the sun and moon that set, they rise again; they die yet reborn again just like the passing cycle of the four seasons which repeats itself once more.

Many *fight* against circumstances throughout their lives by opposing all that they deem to be unlovely. Little do they know that their acknowledgement of all these unlovely things around them actually reinforces their existence. Since Vedic scriptures proclaim that *"Yad Bhavam, Tad Bhavati"* (as is the feeling, so is the result), hatred, anger and fear are intense feelings that can sustain a specific undesirable reality in this objective world.

The Trinity greatly revered by the Hindus - Lord Brahma, Lord Vishnu and Lord Shiva, are in fact the personification of the creative process. Brahma is seen as the Creator of the Universe, Vishnu the Sustainer and Shiva the destroyer. The cycle of creation, sustenance and destruction repeats itself every single moment in one's mind. Experiences, the reflection of one's thoughts, define one's reality and are *sustained* with continuous attention. When a new idea is borne in the mind of man, the old concept of the self is *destroyed* to pave way for a newer experienced reality.

Because memory is fallible, man very often does not remember the thoughts he has dwelled upon in the past that were responsible in drawing to him his current experiences. Therefore, do not sustain those unlovely images in your mind by dwelling upon them. Do not join groups that were established to rebel against an unwanted situation. Doing so will only channel more energy to sustain that undesirable state in your mind, which will in turn shape into your current reality. Instead, turn to your wonderful human imagination to correct the situation. Revise these images in your mind as how you would like to experience it in the flesh and the old concept must die to pave way for the new.

Tapping into the subconscious mind opens one to unlimited possibilities. You will never be denied (*impoverished*) of the ideal you would like to experience in your life. This power that you draw from the Self can never be *exhausted* and just like the *sun* and *moon*, even if you experience any failure in life, you can rise again simply by changing the state of your mind. The cycle of the creative process (*creating, sustaining* and *destroying*) is constantly repeating itself.

The Bible states that *"except you be born again, you cannot enter the kingdom of heaven"* (John 3:3). In this world of duality, as there can be no light without darkness, there can also be no birth without death. Therefore, to be 'born' again, you must 'die'; this is Law. You 'die' by discarding your current beliefs regarding your circumstances or even life itself so that you may be lifted to the belief of the ideal that you want to be.

Therefore, although physical action is necessary for man to work towards realising his goals, it is even more important for him to know the Universal Law. When he does, failure can never touch him and he will understand what William

Ernest Henley truly meant when he wrote in his poem 'Invictus', *"I am the master of my fate: I am the captain of my soul"*.

聲不過五，五聲之變，不可勝聽也。色不過五，五色之變，不可勝觀也。味不過五，五味之變，不可勝嘗也。戰勢不過奇正，奇正之變，不可勝窮也。

There are not more than five notes in the musical scale, yet these five notes produce unlimited possible variations of melodies that can ever be heard. There are not more than five primary colours available, yet different combinations reveal endless possible hues that can ever be seen. There are not more than five cardinal tastes, yet when combined produce endless possible flavours that can ever be tasted. Battles are limited to only two measures; direct and indirect, yet their combination creates endless possibilities of securing victory.

The Wu Xing (five phases) theory is very important in the Chinese community as the system is widely used to describe interactions and relationships between phenomena. This theory is applied in many different fields such as geomancy (popularly known as Feng Shui), astrology, traditional Chinese medicine, music, military strategy and even martial arts.

Chinese philosophy believes that the universe is made up of the combination of five elements namely wood, fire, earth, metal and water. Sacred literatures in Hinduism also mentions about the underlying fivefold "gross" elements (ether, air, water, fire and earth) in creation. The Taittirīya Upanishad describes the five "sheaths" of existence, beginning with undifferentiated energy - the Self:

"From this very Atman (the Self) did space come into being; from space, air; from air, fire; from fire, the waters; from the waters, the earth; from the earth, plants; from plants, food; and from food, Man..."

Here, Sun Tzu tries to conjure an image of limitless possibilities derived from the combination of limited sources by citing that unlimited variation of music can be composed from merely *five notes* in the Chinese *musical scale (jué, zhǐ, gōng, shāng* and *yǔ)*, different possible hues can be obtained from the combination of the *five primary colours* (green, red, yellow, white and black) and different flavours can be produced with the combination of the *five cardinal tastes* (sour, bitter, sweet, pungent and salty).

With the combination of the five external senses, one defines his or her life experiences. Since external circumstances are a reflection of one's state of mind, experience your dream fulfilled in your mind's eye as how you would experience it in the flesh. Envision your desire fulfilled by combining your five inner senses of inner sight, sound, scent, taste and touch. Done vividly, you have constructed a structure in the fourth-dimensional plane that will objectify itself in your current reality in good time. The combination of the five inner senses to experience your wish as having been fulfilled will *create* wonders of *endless possibilities* for yourself.

By putting in the necessary effort and tuning into the powers of your mind, *victory* of attaining your goal shall definitely be yours.

奇正相生，如循環之無端，孰能窮之哉！

The forces of direct and indirect measures complement and engender each other. Each being the cause of the other, their cycle is continuous just like a circle that has neither an end nor a beginning.

Both thoughts and actions mutually affect each other. Thoughts influence our actions, and through actions, we draw to ourselves specific circumstances. These circumstances become our experiences, which will in turn mould our thoughts again. The never-ending cycle of action and reaction repeats itself over and over again.

Hindu scriptures tell us that *the same mind is responsible for both liberation and bondage.* Consciousness, which is of pure substance (energy), pervades the entire universe. The Universal Mind too pervades the entire Universe. In fact, the entire Universe is a mere projection of the mind. In other words, the mind is what shapes the pure undifferentiated energy by assuming a particular form. However, the ignorant man is not aware that the mind is the one responsible for the mirage of experiences he now perceives in his life and therefore becomes so easily enslaved by his very own creation. Not knowing better, he becomes attached to the forms projected by his very own mind, which was supposedly his instrument to shape his experienced reality, thus leading him into bondage. Only when man awakens from his deep slumber will he realise the play that is conjured by the mind and be liberated from limited circumstances.

Nonetheless, the cycle of action and reaction can never be broken. In this world of duality, where there is action, there must always be a corresponding reaction and vice versa. If you are filled with negative thoughts, all that can manifest as your experienced reality will only be negative. From experiencing a negative reality, your perception of the situation leads to more negative thoughts to be formed in your mind and the cycle then repeats itself. The cycle continues in the same direction until the awakened man decides to change it by using the intellect to direct the mind to dwell only on thoughts that are worthy of him.

激水之疾，至于漂石者，勢也。鷙鳥之擊，至于毀折者，節也。
是故善戰者，其勢險，其節短，勢如張弩，節如機發。

The rush of fierce water that causes rocks to drift with its flow denotes force. Playing its part in its mission to kill, a hawk strikes to break its prey. Therefore, great warriors are those who possess great power yet are swift, agile and precise in their movements; their potential is likened to that found in a fully drawn bow and their agility and precision are similar to the release of the trigger.

Napoleon Hill believes that *"man alone has the power to transform his thoughts into physical reality"*. Sun Tzu uses various metaphors to illustrate the image of force or power such as that of *rushing fierce water, the striking of a hawk, a solid rock casted on a fragile egg* and *rolling boulders from a mountain* (last verse of this chapter).

A great warrior of the mind is a man who possesses persistence and a strong willpower. His willpower is forceful just like that of *rushing fierce water that causes rocks to drift with its flow*. This means that he will allow no obstacles to hinder his journey in objectifying his ideal.

Also, just like a hawk, the Man on a mission to externalise his goals wastes no time by dwelling on uncertainties and doubts. He does not hesitate nor does he struggle to act to achieve his targets.

The inner power possessed by a warrior is likened to the potential power found in *a fully drawn bow*, ready to be released in any direction. His precise judgment and one-pointedness on the other hand is visible in the release of the trigger.

Spirit is infinite and ever flowing and it is the mind of man that expresses the Spirit into form. Equipped with a strong willpower, you are like a *fully drawn bow*, ready to set yourself a goal to strike. The release of the trigger conjures an image of one-pointedness. The advice behind the act is for you to remain one-pointed in the goal that you have set for yourself. Therefore, affix your vision on that goal and do not allow your attention to divert to anything else until the fulfilment of it.

One can follow the example of Arjuna, the great devotee of Lord Krishna in Hinduism when he and some other disciples were tested for their power of concentration. With their bows and arrows, they were supposed to shoot the eye of a bird off a tree. When the first disciple was called, he was asked as to what he could see from his position. The disciple went on to list that he could see the other birds perching on that same tree and even the other fellow disciples standing on the ground. Displeased with his answer, the teacher ordered the student to back off.

When it came to Arjuna's turn, Arjuna came forth with an answer so different from that which the other princes have expected. Arjuna said, *"My dear Sir! I can see nothing but the eye, which is to be my target! If you ask me whether the eye belongs to a bird or to a beast, I am not in a position to reply as I see only the eye and nothing but the eye alone!"*

Now this is what we call one-pointedness. With such precision, it is impossible for you to be swayed from your target. Accompanied with a strong willpower, you are sure to hit it!

紛紛紜紜，鬥亂，而不可亂也。渾渾沌沌，形圓，而不可敗也。亂生于治，怯生于勇，弱生于強。治亂，數也。勇怯，勢也。強弱，形也。

Amidst chaos, although there appears to be havoc and disorder, there is no confusion. Although troops appear as though they are moving in circles in turmoil of a battle, it is not an indication for defeat. Remember that disorder is in fact, derived from order, cowardice from courage and weakness from strength. It is upon the assessment of a situation that one concludes the existence of order or disorder. Cowardice or courage is denoted by force, and whether one appears weak or strong is just a matter of appearance.

Nothing is what it seems. The entire Universe consists of only pure consciousness that is undifferentiated into any form. This is known as the *Atma* (the Self). All forms of creation are a mirage within a multi-faceted dream. In fact, our existence is just a dream within a dream.

All the forms that the senses perceive are merely projections of the mind and are transient in nature. However, the root substance of the Self remains changeless and eternal. Although the Self is a witness to man's fleeting experiences, it is untouched by them.

The Universe is governed by the Universal Law. Regardless of man's circumstances, the Law just is and there is no room for *confusion*. Unbiased like the sun that shines light on all, the Law too is impartial and operates the same way for everyone regardless of their background, race or creed. It is only through the Law that man draws to himself, either positive or negative, experiences of reality. As highlighted in Chapter 1, remember that Order is Heaven's first law. Any seeming *disorder* that you perceive to exist in your life's circumstances is actually derived from and governed by *order* (the Law).

Regardless of your current circumstances, however negative they may appear to be, persevere. Even if your life seems to be turning in circles and there seems to be no way out of the situation, it is not an indication for *defeat*. Everyone has the same potential within to be the person whom they dream of being. The Law is unmoved by circumstances and you can still live the life that you desire so long you cultivate faith in the Self.

The key is to select a scene that would indicate the most natural outcome following the fulfilment of your dream. Imagine the scene as vividly as you can in your mind's eye. Confine your imagination to play out only the selected scene over and over again until you drift off to sleep every night. You are to be faithful to your imaginary act until you experience it in your outer world. The vision *"has its own appointed hour; it ripens and it will flower. If it be long, then wait, for it is sure and it will not be late."* (Habakkuk 2:3)

The world that man sees is that of duality. Already mentioned previously, this world of duality cannot allow the existence of something without its counterpart. Just as light cannot exist without darkness, order can also not exist without disorder, so do courage without cowardice and strength without weakness.

Whether your life appears to be in *order* or *disorder*, the fault lies not with circumstances but your own vision. Only one who possesses clarity of mind can understand and appreciate the *order* (governed by the Law) that the Universe operates with.

Some people have the *courage* to go after their dreams whereas some do not. The willpower to succeed in reaching out for the stars is significantly stronger in those who are *courageous* than those who are deemed *cowards*. What separates these two types of people is merely the different degree of exercising the same inner *force*. *Cowardice* is merely allowing fear to obstruct one's *courage*. Remember that FEAR is really only "False Evidences Appearing Real".

Therefore, true strength lies within the mind of man. Whether he be *strong* or *weak*, it does not depend on what he portrays without but what he really is within. Therefore, judge not a book by its cover for external appearances can be deceiving. A *strong* man is verily one who has mastered his mind. He allows no possibility of failure to exist within his consciousness.

故善動敵者，形之，敵必從之；予之，敵必取之；以利動之，以實待之。

Therefore, those who are skilled at aggravating the enemy will deceive them with appearances of which they know the enemy will react to; they offer something that the enemy will be tempted to catch hold of. The skilled warrior lures the enemy to react as he awaits them to seize the bait.

A good warrior of the mind is one who is unmoved by temptations that will steer him or her away from the vision.

As already mentioned in the paragraph before, a strong man will allow no possibility of failure to exist within his consciousness as he strives to perfect his exercise of willpower. The noble man challenges himself not by avoiding temptations, but by placing temptations before him to *lure the 'enemy'* that exist within him to nip them in the bud before they become more strongly rooted in his consciousness.

Let's take the example of people who want to be a vegetarian. Just because one is entrapped within a community that strictly adheres to a vegetarian diet does not reflect one's determination in giving up a meat-eating diet. It is only when they are exposed to the temptations of meat that they will truly know the degree of willpower that they possess in becoming a vegetarian.

Just like how one must shake the nail on the wall to ensure that it is strong enough to hold the frame of a picture that is to be hung, you must also constantly keep yourself in check to see if you possess a strong willpower and unwavering faith to withstand the challenges that may come in your way to secure your ideal. If you still find yourself reacting to circumstances that suggest to you the impossibility of your dream, then you are still doubtful about the power of the Law. The day when you can *'see no evil'*, *'hear no evil'* and *'speak no evil'* (shutting your five external senses to all that stray you from your inner vision), your dream is sure to materialise on this objective plane.

Therefore, do not run away from the temptations that are placed before you. Robert G. Ingersoll was correct when he said that *"the great thing is to make people intelligent enough and strong enough, not to keep away from temptation, but to resist it"*.

When the inner enemy is aroused as it *seizes the bait* of temptations, immediately eradicate them from your consciousness. Find strength in the Universal Law that cannot fail you. Remind yourself of your vision and meditate on it. With unwavering faith, your will must come to pass.

故善戰者，求之于勢，不責于人，故能擇人任勢；任勢者，其戰人也，如轉木石，木石之性，安則靜，危則動，方則止，圓則行。故善戰人之勢，如轉圓石于千仞之山者，勢也。

Ultimately, a good warrior is one who knows that the secret of battle lies not in individuals but the harnessing of potential force. Hence, appoint those who can be entrusted with the proper utilisation of force; their presence in the battlefield is likened to the rolling of logs and boulders. The nature of a log or boulder is that they remain still when positioned on flat ground, but will start rolling down when released from a dangerous steep slope. Therefore, warriors who know how to harness force will possess the potential power that is similar to the rolling boulders from a mountain of one thousand ren high.

Ultimately, man who is the Master of his mind knows that the secret of objectifying an ideal does not lie with external circumstances but with the harnessing of potential energy.

As stated in Chapter 1, preserving the Rule is extremely important in the mastery of the mind. Sun Tzu's advice of *appointing those who can be entrusted with the proper utilisation of force* is to allocate the governing power to the fight faculty. Know who the Master really is (i.e. the Self). Assuming the role as the Master, use your intellect to direct the mind, which will in turn control your senses to dwell only on ideals that are worthy of you.

You should already understand by now that the Universe is made up of nothing but pure energy. This energy, in its original state, is the undifferentiated formless substance of life. Just like *the nature of a log or boulder*, this substance remains *still* without the presence of mental activity for it is the mind that differentiates it into various forms.

Therefore, the awakened man is one who is aware of the Universal Law and abides by the Rule. He possesses a strong momentum similar to that of *rolling logs and boulders from a mountain of one thousand ren high* as he *properly utilises* the creative process in manifesting his vision in this third-dimensional world.

6 - 虛實

THE ACTUAL SITUATION

孫子曰：凡先處戰地而待敵者佚，後處戰地而趨戰者勞。

Sun Tzu said: Generally, the one who reaches the battlefield first can await the enemy with confidence; the one who reaches later will struggle as they hasten themselves to fight.

Sun Tzu's phrase of one "(reaching) *the battlefield*" *first* signifies *confidence* and readiness to undertake a mission of great importance. To do this, turn away from your senses and faithfully rely on your inner vision. The real battle with undesirable circumstances does not lie with physical struggle but within your mind. Revise all the unlovely scenes in your mind's eye and see life the way you desire it to be. Then, wait with *confidence* for the seed you have planted to grow and flower. Your current reality that you now deem your *enemy* will soon become your friend.

Those who do not require any catalyst to turn inward to seek for strength are those who possess *confidence* in the Self, and inspired from the Source, they act. Otherwise, most people have the tendency to react to their negative circumstances. Failing to *reach* out to the actual *battlefield* in their minds, they react to their physical experiences and thus *struggle as they hasten themselves to fight.*

故善戰者，致人而不致于人。能使敵人自至者，利之也；能使敵不得至者，害之也。

Therefore, a skilled warrior is one who is able to impose his will on the enemy, but does not allow the enemy's will to be imposed on him. It is with the use of bait that the warrior is able to summon the enemy's presence before him. One is also able to make the enemy withdraw by showing signals of potential harm.

The man who is *skilled* in the art of mastering the mind will never allow negative circumstances to buoy him. He rejects from his mind the reality of all experiences that do not please him and envisions life exactly the way he desires it to be. That is how he *imposes his will on the enemy* instead of allowing the *enemy's will to be imposed on him.*

It is from our life experiences that we learn to exercise our power of discrimination to decide the states that the mind should dwell on. Experiences are nothing but lessons to direct man towards realising the infinite power that lies latent within him. Henry B. Wilson said, *"he who finds diamonds must grapple in mud and mire because diamonds are not found in polished stones."* Our life experiences are the trigger to our reactions. It is from our reactions that we will know the extent of our faith in the Self. Experiences are nothing but baits for man to *summon the enemy's presence before him* (the enemy symbolises negative emotions such as doubts, fear and anxiety) so that he can remove them from his consciousness and allow the light of the Self to shine forth. Therefore, braving through the different challenges and temptations in life gives us the opportunity to reassess our progress towards realising our true nature.

The universe is built upon the foundation of collective beliefs and is sustained by them. This foundation is derived from ego-consciousness with ideas revolving around lack and impossibility. In this context, societal beliefs and norms are your *enemy*.

Your current experience only persists if your beliefs remain the same. If you want a difference experience, you will then have to change the course of your mind. Convicted in your ideals as you choose not to succumb to society's set of beliefs as to what is and what is not possible to achieve in life, you are sending out *signals of potential harm* to its already established structure. The moment you reap the fruit of your faith, you will silent all naysayers who once told you that you could not achieve the goal. You will also prove that man is never bound by manmade laws. If you dream big enough, you are sure to set a new precedent. What was once deemed impossible will now be accepted by others as possible. That is why Anthony Robbins says: *"If you always do what you have always done, you will always get what you have always got."*

故敵佚能勞之，飽能飢之，安能動之。

So, when the enemy appears to be idle, toil them; when well fed, starve them; and when the enemy is calm, aggravate them.

Remove doubts, fear, anxiety and any other negative feelings that do not reflect the glory of the Self from your consciousness. Deal with them harshly. Do not allow any impurity to taint your mind or sleep within you. The process of purifying the mind is a rigorous one. As mentioned in the previous paragraph, test yourself to see if you still react negatively to circumstances. Assess your feelings for each experience to determine your progress.

Man usually thinks he is perfect until something comes along to trigger his dark side. Until then, the negative qualities remain dormant within him.

出其所不趨，趨其所不意；行千里而不勞者，行于無人之地也；攻而必取者，攻其所不守也；守而必固者，守其所不攻也。故善攻者，敵不知其所守；善守者，敵不知其所攻。

Go to a place where the enemy must rush to defend, and hasten yourself to places where the enemy least expects you to be. To march over one thousand li without distress, one must march through a trail of no man. The one who wants to succeed in attacking should attack where the enemy is unable to defend. On the other hand, to ensure that one's defence is solid means that one must defend oneself in places so that it becomes impossible for the enemy to attack. Therefore, the enemy will not know where to defend against a warrior who is skilful in the art of attack.

Similarly, the enemy will also not know how to attack an army that is skilled in defence.

To *go to a place where the enemy must rush to defend* is to break the barriers that society has contained you with. Society expects you to conform to established norms and rules. However, this should not be your reason for living a mediocre life. Know that you are an infinite being and ascend beyond the idea of lack and limit.

To *march through a trail of no man* is to turn inward to rely on the power of your imagination. With only your imagination, you can *travel a thousand li* without having to physically move an inch. Assume the state of consciousness you desire to possess even if your reason and outer senses deny its reality. Changing a concept within one's mind is to change physical reality. No one else but you, the Mastermind, knows of the plan. Due to the subconscious influence, the Universe is left with no choice but to yield to your desire when you have saturated your being with the ideal you would like to externalise. Other people who are instrumental to bring your goal into being will be *unable to defend* themselves against this unseen force.

The same principle applies to *defending* your ideals. If you dream of achieving big goals in life, which majority of the people would deem impossible to attain, proclaiming them out loud will just invite ridicule. To remain faithful to your ideals in your mind is to 'pray in secret' where no other people can discover. This will save you from dealing with unnecessary problems and destructive criticisms that may impede your progress towards attaining your ideal. The possibility of you getting discouraged halfway through your journey in securing it is thereby reduced. Therefore, it is best to keep your objectives to yourself instead of sharing them with people who cannot appreciate them. Why surround yourself with people who ridicule your ideas? If they are cynical of your dreams and their cynicism make you feel uncomfortable, then it is time to cut the cord!

The Law of Nature is growth. So do not let pessimistic people stunt your growth. Remember to only surround yourself with people who inspire you to reach out to higher ideals.

微乎微乎！至于無形；神乎神乎！至于無聲，故能為敵之司命。進而不可禦者，衝其虛也；退而不可追者，速而不可及也。

Profound indeed is the art of invisibility and how mysterious is the art of silence that when both are perfected, make one the master of the enemy's fate. To barge into the enemy's territory, attack their weakest points so that they cannot defend themselves. On the other hand, if one's army needs to be withdrawn, ensure that troops move at a pace to make it impossible for the enemy to catch up with.

Silence and invisibility are the two qualities that man must *perfect* if he wants to go beyond his limits. Equipped with both, he shapes his worldly experiences with his mind. Having mastered them, there will be no greater force that can triumph against his will.

There is nothing to fear but fear itself. The weakest point of the people blinded with fear is their fear for change. Therefore, there is no need to engage yourself in idle talk or petty arguments. Withdraw yourself from conflicts immediately as they arise. When faced with an impossible situation, detach from your five external senses and return to the realm of your mind to correct the scene. Experience it in your mind the way you had wanted it to be in the flesh and it will shape your future. Otherwise, lamenting and complaining about negative situations will only cause the same pattern to repeat itself again.

故我欲戰，敵雖高壘深溝，不得不與我戰者，攻其所必救也；我不欲戰，雖劃地而守之，敵不得與我戰者，乖其所之也。

Even if the enemy is sheltered by high walls and deep moats, they will be left with no choice but to yield to our wish to fight if we attack at positions where they are obliged to protect. If however we do not desire to fight, even if our defence is merely a line drawn on the ground, we can still prevent a battle from happening if we successfully mislead them.

Man's will is strong. This paragraph reinforces the notion that we should not be enslaved by what our five external senses perceive. Instead of remaining passive and be buoyed by circumstances, assume responsibility over your experiences. Know that the power lies within you.

However solid the foundation of society's beliefs is (whether *sheltered by high walls and deep moats*), they can still be shattered. Witnessing your ability to achieve the goals that people once believed to be impossible will leave others at awe over the vigour and confidence that you possess to live the life of your dreams. They are then left battling within themselves, wondering why they could not do the same.

There is no need to convince these naysayers about your beliefs of attaining the impossible. There is no better evidence than the example of your life. Have faith in your vision, just be yourself and carry on with your daily chores. You will subconsciously influence the right people to bring your goal into reality. The people around you are just a reflection of yourself. Although they may be *misled* to think that they were acting out of their own freewill, it was you, the divine tactician, who was responsible for their actions.

故形人而我無形，則我專而敵分，我專為一，敵分為十，是以十攻其一也。則我眾而敵寡，能以眾擊寡，則我之所與戰者，約矣。

Therefore, to be able to unravel the enemy's plans while ours remain concealed, our forces are concentrated whilst the enemy's is divided. With a concentrated force, our power therefore becomes ten times stronger than that of the enemy's, which we can then use to effectively attack them. Battling the enemy's inferior force with a superior one can definitely restrict the enemy's ability to fight back.

While everyone else is busy with the hustle and bustle of their life, plant a seed (thought) in the divine garden (your mind) and wait for it to grow. Be discreet about your *plan* before your vision materialises on this objective plane. Speak to no one about your dream. Concentrate all your attention on your vision to harness force until it is so great that it can alter your current physical reality. All that are not in harmony with your thoughts will somehow make way for you. When you possess faith and a strong willpower to objectify your ideals, the entire world will be unable to resist your subconscious influence that compels them to behave in certain ways to bring your goals into reality.

吾所與戰之地不可知，不可知，則敵所備者多，敵所備者多，則我所與戰者寡矣。故備前則後寡，備後則前寡，備左則右寡，備右則左寡，無所不備，則無所不寡。寡者，備人者也；眾者，使人備己者也。

Where we intend to attack the enemy should not be made known to them. If they do not know where we are going to attack them, the enemy will have to prepare themselves for all possibilities, thus spreading their resources thin in many different directions. This would mean that the potential obstacles that will lie in our way to conquer the enemy will be less for if they focus on defending the front, their back will be weak. If they prepare themselves to defend the back, the front will be weak. To defend the left, the right will be weak and to focus on defending the right, the left will be weak. So, if troops are sent to defend every possible locations of attack, all of their bases will be weak. Weak are those who need to prepare to defend themselves from possible attacks. The strong ones are those whose power can compel the opponent to prepare to defend against them.

Sun Tzu cannot stress enough on the importance of remaining discreet about one's desires and mental actions. Rearranging circumstances in your mind gives no room for anyone else to resent your vision until it materialises in your physical experience.

This paragraph also suggests that baseless *defence* without proper strategy is nothing but a futile attempt. Do not be moved by other people's criticisms. Just because they do not believe in your dreams does not mean that your dreams are not achievable. Reacting to their criticisms only shows that you possess a poor mental stamina and thus, motivate them to taunt you further. Remain composed and take control of the situation by turning inward. This is how you demonstrate fortitude and confidence in your vision. Always wanting to preserve established norms and ideas, society will become afraid that their long belief system may be flawed. So, they will be *compelled* to *defend against* yours.

"Everything that irritates us about others can lead us to an understanding of ourselves." (Carl Jung)

故知戰之地，知戰之日，則可千里而會戰。不知戰地，不知戰日，則左不能救右，右不能救左，前不能救後，後不能救前，而況遠者數十里，近者數里乎？

Therefore, the one who knows the place and time of the upcoming battle can march even a thousand li to fight. However, the one who knows not of both will be weak in defence as the troop that guards the left cannot help save the ones who guard the right, and the right also cannot help defend the ones on the left; the front army cannot rescue the back, and the troops at the back cannot rush in time to aid the front. This is true even for troops who are separated by near distances of merely a few li, so how much more so if the troops are separated by great distances of tens of li?

If you are clear about your goal, you will have the willpower to *march even a thousand li* to fight for it. However, if you do not know for sure what you really want to achieve, you will be easily dissuaded by criticisms and discouragement in pursuing your goal. This is true to move even a finger (*merely a few li*: a small goal), how much more so when working towards a bigger one (*separated by great distances of tens of li*)?

以吾度之，越人之兵雖多，亦奚益于勝哉？故曰：勝可為也，敵雖眾，可使無鬥。

According to my opinion, why should having troops of a large number be an advantage for the people of the Yue Kingdom in attaining victory? I say that victory can still be secured even if the enemy's army is larger than ours as we can make them incapable of fighting.

It is not important whether you have all the necessary resources to bring your dreams into reality. Despite being surrounded with plenty of resources, if you do not know how to use them, they are still useless. Sun Tzu suggests that *victory can still be secured* even if the opposing force is larger than yours. Even if one million people are against you, you can still succeed!

Despite the fact that the Yue Kingdom had superior manpower to the Wu Kingdom in ancient China, Wu still won majority of the battles. Having more is not necessarily better. Your ability to optimise the resources available will determine your success. Make the best out of everything that you have, be it physical resources or mental strength, and you are bound to be successful.

故策之而知得失之計，作之而知動靜之理，形之而知死生之地，角之而知有餘不足之處。故形兵之極，至于無形；無形，則深間不能窺，智者不能謀。因形而措勝于眾，眾不能知，人皆知我所以勝之形，而莫知吾所以制勝之形；故其戰勝不復，而應形於無窮。

Therefore, the plan is to estimate the enemy's gains and losses. Probe them so that you may learn the reasons behind their actions. Make the enemy reveal the factors that can strengthen and weaken their force. Compare the enemy's troops to ours to determine the aspects of which we are superior and inferior to them. The ultimate skill that an army must master is that of invisibility; the art of invisibility hinders others from prying into our deepest secrets so that even the wisest of man cannot plot against us. By observing the enemy's tactics without their knowledge, one can gain victory even if their army is larger. All men can see the tactics of which I conquer them with, but they will never know the strategy that I have used that led us to such victory. Therefore, never repeat the tactics that have been used in the past to secure a victory. Instead, the strategies one employ to respond to circumstances should be inexhaustible.

The way to do it is to fully understand the nature of your mind and ego. Enquire the Self and examine the activities of the mind. Identify the thoughts and feelings that sustain your current situation and remove them from your mind.

Assess and determine for yourself how much of society's limited beliefs that you believe to be true. How have you subjected yourself to those beliefs?

List down all your strengths and weaknesses to get a clear picture of those qualities that serve you and those that do not. Be grateful for your strengths and deal with your weaknesses accordingly. If one of your weaknesses is fear to tread on unfamiliar grounds, then remind yourself how much opportunity you could miss out for not doing so.

"Man cannot discover new oceans unless he has the courage to lose sight of the shore." (Andre Gide)

Again, Sun Tzu reminds to keep the knowledge of your strengths and weaknesses, and your master plan to achieve your ideal life (your *deepest secrets*) solely to yourself. This will save you from unnecessary frustrations resulting from others *plotting against* your plans to succeed.

Be ever watchful of your mental activity. Observe the patterns of your thoughts and feelings. Preserve favourable patterns, but discard those that are not. No matter how strong the negative patterns are rooted in your mind, you can uproot them by replacing them with positive ones. Practicing thinking positive thoughts over a period of time will become a habit and thus, a new pattern is formed.

The society also operates with an existing pattern. Disregard any pattern that is not in harmony with your feeling. When you use your mind to visualise your ideals to bring them into being on this physical plane, you are prompted from within to take certain decisions and behave in a certain way that will bring you towards the materialisation of your vision. However, others can only witness your physical actions and conclude, based on their observation with their five external senses, the pattern that they thought had contributed to your success. They can see the *tactics* which you have used to conquer a mundane life *but they will never know the strategy that you have used that led you to such victory.*

Be as creative as possible. Engage all your five inner senses to concentrate on your goal. Remain steadfast to your vision until it objectifies on this third-dimensional plane. Be open-minded to new possibilities and new ways of doing things.

Remember that if you repeat a pattern that did not serve you in the past, it will not start serving you now. When you have surrendered the ideal to the Self, a way will be made and circumstances will begin to change. You will be prompted from within to take the right actions that will lead you to your goal.

夫兵形象水，水之形，避高而趨下：兵之形，避實而擊虛；水因地而制流，兵因敵而制勝。故兵無常勢，水無常形；能因敵變化而取勝，謂之神。故五行無常勝，四時無常位，日有短長，月有死生。

Military strategies are similar to the nature of water. Water flows by rushing downwards, avoiding high lands to reach the low. So, an army also avoids confronting the strong but attacks the weak. Just like how the nature of ground determines the movement of water, soldiers also carve their victory according to the enemy whom they fight against. Therefore, similar to water that has no permanent form; an army also faces no preset conditions. One who is able to adapt to the enemy's circumstances to secure victory is verily like God. None of the five elements of water, fire, wood, metal and earth is ever predominant. Each of the four seasons also takes their turn to arrive and leave. There are times when the days are short, but at other times, long. The moon also wanes and waxes.

The paragraph suggests that one learns the lesson from the flexible nature of water. To be rigid in one's ways often prevents one from seeing the larger picture. You must learn to adapt to different situations accordingly.

Bruce Lee says to "*be like water making its way through cracks. Do not be assertive, but adjust to the object and you shall find a way around or through it. If nothing within you stays rigid, outward things will disclose themselves. Empty your mind; be formless and shapeless like water. If you put water into a cup, it becomes the cup. You put water into a bottle and it becomes the bottle. You put it in a teapot, it will become the teapot. Now, water can flow or it can crash. Be water, my friend.*"

This is what Spirit is – like water. Man is reminded in the Bile that "*except ye be born of water and the spirit, ye can in no wise enter the kingdom of heaven*". Spirit is infinite and ever flowing, and it is the mind of man that expresses the Spirit into form. It is nothing but a potential field of undifferentiated and formless energy, which takes a form based on the ideas you have in your mind. The "*nature of ground*" that Sun Tzu mentions refers to your mental state. According to the states that you dwell on in your mind, this pure energy will be differentiated into forms on the objective plane that reflect your inner beliefs.

Nothing in this world is permanent. Only Spirit is. Everything that you experience will come to an end one day regardless of whether it is good or bad. If you do not like what you are experiencing in life, change the ideas within and you will witness the change without.

7 - 軍爭

MILITARY STRIVE

孫子曰：凡用兵之法，將受命于君，合軍聚眾，交和而舍，莫難于軍事。軍爭之難者，以迂為直，以患為利。故迂其途，而誘之以利，後人發，先人至，此知迂直之計者也。故軍爭為利，軍爭為危。

Sun Tzu said: The principle rules of leading an army are that the General is to execute the commands of the monarch, raise troops and to pitch camps. There is nothing more challenging than managing military affairs. The army that strives to overcome difficulties must unravel deceptions and turn adversities into advantages. Therefore, confuse the enemy by sending them round in circles and entice them using baits of advantages. Those who are

99

well-versed with the stratagem of deviation can arrive at the destination first even if they began their journey later. Therefore, military strive is about securing advantages and overcoming danger.

According to Sun Tzu, the first *principle rule* in the art of mastering the mind is to listen to the inner calling of the Self. Most people just do what is expected of them even though they know that they are unhappy doing it. However, they are unaware that their motivation behind doing something actually affects their performance level. People usually excel when they do the things that they love over those that they are forced to do. Robert Kiyosaki is right when he says that *"passion is a powerful force. Passion properly directed is unstoppable."*

Take a look at some of the most successful personalities in the world. What is the first thing that crosses your mind when you hear the names of Henry Ford, Bill Gates, Henry J. Kaiser, Charles Lindebergh and F. W. Woolworth? We see them not as people who have amassed a fortune but people who have achieved something great in their lives as they have surpassed the boundaries of what is thought possible by the rest of society. They are where they are today because they simply did the things that they were passionate about and excelled in them. Many think that money is what will make them happy, but money is actually just the resulting factor and not a determinant of success!

Therefore, discover the purpose of your life by listening to your inner voice. This voice can be heard only in silence; when the mind is free from its constant chatter. Rumi says that *"the quieter you become, the more you are able to hear."* The ideas that make you smile are those that resonate with your heart and if you pursue them with faith and determination, you are sure to succeed.

Once you have identified your life purpose, prepare yourself for the journey. Focus all your energy on that goal (*raise troops*).

There is no greater *challenge* than to discipline the mind. The *challenge* for man to objectify his ideals is to withstand any opposing ideas that deny him of it. He must ensure that he continuously dwells on the state that his wish is already fulfilled so that the idea gets impregnated (*pitch camps*) on his subconscious mind.

Man's efforts will succeed only when he *strives to overcome difficulties* by 'seeing' things the way he wants them to be instead of being *deceived* by the appearance of his undesirable circumstances. This is how he will *"turn adversities into advantages"*.

If your monkey mind begins to wander away from the goal, remind yourself of the advantages that follow the fulfilment of the desire (*using baits*). Construct a scene that implies the wish fulfilled and repeat it in your mind (*sending them round in circles*) until you can feel that it is already part of your reality.

Therefore, *those who are well-versed with the stratagem of deviating* the mind from its endless activities to focus only on one goal need not be hasty for *"the vision has its own appointed hour and ... it is sure and will not be late."* (Habakkuk 2:3)

All that man has to do to become the Master of his fate is to constantly keep his focus on the *advantages* that will follow the fulfilment of his desire and to *overcome the dangers* of falling prey to a negative thoughts and feelings.

舉軍而爭利，則不及；委軍而爭利，則輜重捐。是故卷甲而趨，日夜不處，倍道兼行，百里而爭利，則擒三將軍，勁者先，疲者後，其法十一而至；五十里而爭利，則蹶上將軍，其法半至；卅里而爭利，則三分之二至。是故軍無輜重則亡，無糧食則亡，無委積則亡。故不知諸侯之謀者，不能豫交；不知山林、險阻、沮澤之形者，不能行軍，不能鄉導者，不能得地利。

To ensure that the whole army is present to secure an advantage will make one arrive too late. Reducing the size of the army in order to secure an advantage however will require one to abandon important military supply wagons. So, to roll-up one's metal armour and hasten oneself day and night without rest to march double the usual distance, one hundred li away, to secure an advantage will lead to the capture of the Generals of the three divisions as the strong will arrive at the destination first while the weak, later. With this plan, only one-tenth of the original army will arrive at the desired destination. On the other hand, marching fifty li to secure an advantage will cause the top General to fall and only half of the army will arrive at the destination, while marching thirty li for the same objective will result in the safe arrival of two-thirds of the army. An army without its important military supply wagon will lose, so will one without food provisions and supplies. Therefore, those who do not know the strategy of other feudal lords cannot secure their alliances. Those who are not familiar with the terrains of the mountains, forests, defiles, gorges and wetlands cannot lead their troops through them. Not employing native guides, one cannot benefit from the natural advantages that the grounds can offer.

In this paragraph, Sun Tzu discusses the importance of weighing all factors before coming to a decision for any given situation because every decision bears a risk.

If man is to solely rely on his physical efforts and not change his negative mindset, there will surely be missed opportunities as he has not yet realised his role as a divine tactician but instead, believes that he is only a puppet of circumstances. He who simply wishes for an ideal to come true without actually devoting his mind to securing it possesses a weak willpower. A strong volition, and not mere fanciful thinking, is necessary to withstand the journey of working towards one's goal.

Haste is due to the lack of faith. The longer the journey to manifest a particular goal, the stronger the willpower you will require. People with a weak mental stamina are more likely to give up halfway through working towards their goals when they see no sign of progress. They are slaves of the senses.

Therefore, those unequipped with a strong willpower will definitely *lose* the battle. Those who do not know about the nature of the mind are also unable to use it to help them in materialising the life experiences that they desire.

Nothing is impossible. Whenever you doubt of your capability in achieving any particular goal, search for examples of the people who have already succeeded in doing the things that you want to do. Remind yourself that if they can do it, so can you. Just because you have never experienced that vibrational frequency before does not mean it is out of your reach. Reading the stories of successful people can help you map out your path so that you have an idea of the steps that you must take in order to reach where they are.

故兵以詐立，以利動，以分合為變者也，故其疾如風，其徐如林，侵掠如火，不動如山，難知如陰，動如雷霆。掠鄉分眾，廓地分利，懸權而動，先知迂直之計者勝，此軍爭之法也。

And so, an army operates on the basis of deception, acts on the basis of advantages and is transformed through division or combination. An army must therefore be as swift as the wind, remain composed and calm at all times like the forest, invade and plunder the enemy like fire, be unmoved and unshaken by circumstances like the mountain, remain discreet and unpredictable like that of the female nature and strike the enemy like the sound of thunder.

Having plundered the countryside, the goods are to be shared with the troops. To expand one's territory, distribute properly the benefits throughout the area. One is to carefully analyse the situation before acting. Those well-versed with the stratagem of deviation are bound to be victorious. This is the art of military strive.

The harness of Universal force *"operates on the basis of deception"*. It cannot be stressed enough that you are to reject from your mind any circumstances that your five physical senses perceive as real so long they do not conform to your inner vision. Man's *actions* are guided by the ideas he hold onto within his mind. It is therefore important for him to be selective of his thoughts and the states that he chooses to dwell on.

Here, Sun Tzu provides us the criteria of how man should be if he is to manifest his desires using various metaphors. To be *"as swift as the wind"* is to not be rigid in one's ways. Set an objective in your mind, believe that it is already yours and release it. Do not worry how you are going to reach your destination. Just follow the course that your faith brings you to. Even if you do have an initial strategy as to how you will go about to achieve your goal, do not hesitate to tread on another possible path that may also bring you to your destination. Be willing to bend your ways to accept something new. Open-mindedness is the key here.

The wind also does not allow anything to get in its way. So, learn the spirit of fighting from the wind and never be discouraged just because there are obstacles in your way.

"*Notice that the stiffest tree is most easily cracked, while the bamboo or willow survives by bending with the wind.*" (Bruce Lee)

One of the secrets of life is to keep a tranquil mind. Man should never be moved by his circumstances. A tranquil mind is derived from faith. If he has faith in his vision, he will "*be unmoved and unshaken by circumstances like the mountain*".

Do not rush. Your desire is already granted. Take a step back and live your life as though it were and, although time beats slowly on this plane of existence, confirmation of the state you dwell within your mind will surely come in good time. Remember that the Universal force will always work in the most harmonious ways to bring you to your desired goal. So, cultivate patience as haste makes waste. Bad decisions are usually made in haste. A clear mind is therefore necessary to help you make wise decisions as the decisions you make today will shape your tomorrow. So, remain "*composed and calm at all times*" to ensure that you make the best decisions to shape a desirable future.

Also ensure that you safeguard your mind from any negative suggestions that defy the reality of your vision. Do not give in to the temptations that will distort your path in manifesting your goals. Show no mercy to traces of doubts and fear as you eradicate them from your thoughts. This is how you "*invade and plunder the enemy like fire*".

To be *discreet* and *unpredictable like that of the female nature* is to conceal your wishes. Speak to no man about your desires for you are advised in the Bible to *"pray to your Father which is in secret and your Father which is in secret shall reward you openly"* (Matthew 6:6). This will help you avoid any unnecessary opposing forces from sceptics until your pursuit has proven its worth. Once you have visualised in your mind's eye the solution to your problem, surrender the desire to the subconscious mind and wait for it to objectify on this physical plane. March on fearlessly and demonstrate an overwhelming determination *"just like the sound of thunder"* to conquer your problems and be the Master of your fate.

軍政曰：「言不相聞，故為金鼓；視不相見，故為旌旗。」夫金鼓旌旗者，所以一人之耳目也；人既專一，則勇者不得獨進，怯者不得獨退，此用眾之法也。故夜戰多火鼓，晝戰多旌旗，所以變人之耳目也。

The Book of Military Administration says: "The intention of the speaker is not always accurately received by the recipient, thus the need for the use of drums and gongs, and as troops cannot be easily differentiated during a battle, there is a need for flags and pennants."

Drums, gongs, flags and pennants are the means by which one's ears and eyes are unified; when the army is united with a single purpose, the brave cannot advance alone nor can the coward retreat alone. This is how we can effectively manage a large army of men. Therefore, make use of fire and drums during a night battle to influence the ears and eyes of the army, while for battles taking place during the day, use as many flags and pennants as one can.

The arrangement of the Universe is driven by one word - "*intention*". Thinking of something that you would like to achieve is to put forward an *intention*.

Intent is not always communicated effectively to the subconscious mind. Vague imagery leads to vague results. Man must imagine as vividly as he can during his visualisation process to objectify his ideals. Engage all the five senses to work in *unison* when constructing a scene that implies fulfilment of the desire. A clear intention influences every faculty of the body and mind to create the desired result.

Purity of vision is verily the unity of man's thoughts, words and deeds working with a *single purpose* in his mission to secure an end that he desires. To direct the senses is how man claims control over his mind. When his thoughts, words and deeds are completely focused solely on attaining a specific goal, he is meditating on it. Such is the practice of *ekagratha* (one-pointedness) by which everything becomes possible.

故三軍可奪氣，將軍可奪心。是故朝氣銳，晝氣惰，暮氣歸；故善用兵者，避其銳氣，擊其惰歸，此治氣者也。以治待亂，以靜待譁，此治心者也。以近待遠，以佚待勞，以飽待飢，此治力者也。

The spirit of all three ranks of the army may be dampened and the top General's motivation may also be lost. It is said that the enthusiasm and energy level of the army are at its peak in the morning; at noon, they become idle; and by evening, the army will only look forward to returning to camp. Therefore, one who is skilled in the art of war will avoid battling with the enemy whose soldiers' motivation is at its highest peak, but will attack them when they are exhausted. This is what we call the art of manipulating the mood of the enemy's army.

The army is to maintain discipline while awaiting chaos to strike the enemy – this is the way to ensure that the army remains composed. Remain near the goal while the enemy is still far away from it, wait at ease while the enemy struggles and be well-fed while the enemy is starving – this is the way to preserve one's strength.

Man's stages of mental activity are represented by a certain timing of the day. It is described to be *at its peak in the morning*, becomes *idle at noon* and slows down tremendously in the evenings, especially when nearing bedtime.

"The breeze at dawn has secrets to tell you. Don't go back to sleep. You must ask for what you really want. Don't go back to sleep." (Rumi)

Those who understand the nature of the mind will know that visualising a desired end when the mind is still actively engaged in all kinds of other thoughts will be a futile attempt. Warriors of the mind will therefore rearrange their experiences only when the mind is still. To rewrite your experiences, immobilise your physical body and induce a state of consciousness similar to sleep. As your body and mind relax, your mental activity is toned down. Then, imagine yourself performing the proposed action that suggests that which you would do in the flesh were you to realise your goal.

This does not necessarily mean that the visualisation process can only be done in the night before bedtime. Man can visualise his ideals anywhere and anytime of the day as long as he silences his mind.

"Make time to listen to your intuition. Your most valuable intuitive wisdom often comes when you are relaxed and open to receiving it." (Jack Canfield)

When you throw a stone into the middle of a pond, you can see ripples spreading out from that point. This is exactly the same with 'consciously willing' for something to happen using the power of your mind. As we are all connected, one thought affects the entire Universe as you introduce your 'will'. The ripples (signature of your 'will') can only be seen and spread out to reach others if the water (the mind) is still. Imagine throwing a stone into a raging ocean, you can be sure that you will never see the trace of where the stone was dropped into it.

So, *discipline* your mind. Anything is possible unto the man who has a disciplined mind. Only when the mind is *disciplined* can the man direct it to work on the goals that he has set for himself; he will be able to properly control his senses to dwell only on the state that he wishes to objectify in his current reality.

With a disciplined mind, you will no longer be trapped in the realm of desires for you know that the desire has already been fulfilled. Man only desires for something when he perceives the goal to be separate from him. Therefore, if you can feel the reality of an experience in your mind as though you are already experiencing it in the flesh even though others are yet to witness its materialisation on this physical plane, it no longer remains a desire but has become a fact since you know that it is already yours.

The disciplined warrior will then *wait at ease* for the objectification of his vision while the whole world around him *struggles* to achieve their goals solely by relying on their physical efforts. This is the hallmark of true spiritual *strength*.

無邀正正之旗，勿擊堂堂之陣，此治變者也；故用兵之法，高陵勿向，背邱勿逆，佯北勿從，銳卒勿攻，餌兵勿食，歸師勿遏，圍師必闕，窮寇勿迫，此用兵之法也。

Avoid battling with an enemy whose flags and pennants are in order and do not attack an army with well-formed troops – this is the way to manage unexpected circumstances; therefore the rules in warfare are to not attack an enemy whose position is on higher grounds or to attack him from behind as he is going downhill. Do not yield to the enemy's pretence of having been defeated and do not attack an enemy who has a burning enthusiasm. One's army is not to swallow the enemy's bait as well as not to withhold an army that is returning to camp. One must leave a way out when surrounding the enemy. Also, do not pressure the enemy that has been cornered. This is what we call by the Art of War.

Sun Tzu advises that you must always be prepared for *unexpected circumstances*. Although man must exert certain force in order reach his goal, he must never impose his beliefs on someone else.

There are a few rules that man must observe when he wishes to re-write his life experiences. It is clear from this paragraph that Sun Tzu stresses on the quality of compassion. While man should continue to fight for his goals and defend his beliefs, he must allow some flexibility in his approaches. There is no need to challenge people who are convicted that their limited beliefs are true. When your ideals have yet to materialise on this physical plane, they will continue to think that their ideas prevail. Why be restless simply because their ideas differ from yours? The world is only a reflection of your inner thoughts and feelings. Nothing changes until you change, but everything changes once you change. If you do not like what you see, then turn within and change it.

There is also no need for you to fight against people who show resentment in your beliefs. They are drowned in their own misery and their lives are *going downhill*. Just because they believe that they cannot make it, they also think that you are one of them.

Cynthia Occelli is correct in saying that "*when people undermine your dreams, predict your doom or criticise you, remember that they are telling you their story, not yours.*"

So, why bother your mind over the things that people say out of ignorance? You will prove your worth one day when your ideals materialise on this physical plane. Until then, persevere in your vision and show compassion to those who are still imprisoned by their limited ideas.

8 - 九變

NINE VARIATIONS

孫子曰：凡用兵之法，將受命于君，合軍聚眾；圮地無舍，衢地合交，絕地無留，圍地則謀，死地則戰，途有所不由，軍有所不擊，城有所不攻，地有所不爭，君命有所不受。故將通于九變之利者，知用兵矣。將不通于九變之利者，雖知地形，不能得地之利矣。治兵不知九變之術，雖知地利，不能得人之用矣。

Sun Tzu said: The principles of warfare to lead an army is for the General to receive the commands from the Ruler and to raise an army; do not camp on difficult grounds, join forces with allies on intersecting grounds, do not linger on dangerous grounds, rely on strategy when the army is on surrounded ground and fight if on deadly ground. There are routes not to be taken, armies not to be fought with, cities not to be attacked, grounds not to be contested for and royal commands that should not be obeyed. The General who understands the nine variations will know how to lead his army. On the other hand, the General who does not comprehend the merits of these principles cannot, even if he is familiar with a particular terrain, fully utilise the terrain to his advantage. Even if the leader of an army knows of favourable locations, he who is unversed with the nine variations technique cannot make the best use of his men.

To conquer the struggles that you face in life, it is important to seek for inner guidance. Listen to your heart and "*receive commands*" from the Self (*the Ruler*) to set your purpose of existence. The ideas that resonate with your being are those that make you feel exhilarated and are worth fighting for. Having ascertained your goals, prepare yourself and take all the necessary steps to bring them into reality. The best *army* to raise to help you conquer your struggles in life is the mind.

Dwelling on *difficulties* do not present you with the solution. Therefore, Sun Tzu advises all not to "*camp on difficult grounds*". When you are struggling with any particular situation, do not allow your mind to occupy that state or the reality you now experience will never change. Instead, direct your senses within to seek for a solution to your problems.

Your best *ally* is your subconscious mind. The outer world is a direct reflection of the ideas and feelings that you hold within you. In other words, all circumstances that you experience are a direct outward result of the ideas imprinted on the subconscious mind. The subconscious mind is what governs our reality. *Joining forces* with it, you can tap into the Universal storehouse of wisdom and knowledge that holds the answers to all of your questions.

Do not allow negative thoughts, emotions and habits to exist within you. If you do, you are *lingering on dangerous ground* and you will only draw to yourself more situations that will further intensify the negativity in your mind.

Have faith in your vision. Whatever goals that you set for yourself, always devise a *strategy* consisting of a series of small steps that will help bring you there. However, famous actor Will Smith reminds that *"there is no reason to have a Plan B because it will only distract your Plan A"*. Therefore, to prepare a backup plan only shows that you have no faith in your original strategy.

When Sun Tzu tells warriors to *"rely on strategy when the army is on surrounded ground"*, he is reminding all to be flexible in their approaches and act according to situation. So, whenever you feel trapped in any undesirable circumstance, remind yourself of the end that you desire. Instead of focusing on your problems, draw your attention back to your vision. If you maintain the faith, the way (*strategy*) will be revealed. You will be prompted from within to act in certain ways that will help bring you out of the situation and redirect you to the path of fulfilling your goal.

Life is what you make out of it. Having objectives is to set a destination for yourself to steer you towards a particular direction in this ocean of life. When you face obstacles along your way that threaten the fulfilment of your ideals, persevere and continue *fighting*. Do not give up on your goals just because you encounter some challenges in your path. Remember that you become wiser and stronger with every obstacle that you overcome. This is what we call by *fighting on deadly ground*.

In pursuit of your goals, you must be very careful not to tread on any path that violates Dharma (righteousness). Those who do not know the nature of the Self believe in a limited Universe. They therefore often resort to unscrupulous means to attain their goals, unaware of the fact that the Universe is in fact abundant with resources. Whenever a resource runs out, the Universal force will replace it with something else. Hence, avoid all *routes* (ideas and practices) that are against the principles of Dharma.

It is also important to perfect the skill of discrimination. You must be able to discern the goals that are worth fighting for from those that are not. Carefully select your ideals. Do not fight just for the sake of fighting. Know exactly what you truly desire and the reason behind it. Ask yourself if the ideal you are fighting for is worthy of you. If it is not, then invest your time and effort in another ideal that is.

For example, you may already have a good house to live in but observing your friends who have bigger houses may compel you to desire to have another house like theirs too. Assess the motivation behind that desire. Does your desire really stem from wanting a bigger house to improve your comfort, or does it stem from jealousy and ego? If the latter is true, then you are operating from feelings of inferiority. You draw unto yourself the experiences that match the frequency of your thoughts and feelings. Affixing this state in your mind will only produce more circumstances to sustain your feeling of inferiority.

Therefore, carefully discern your motives. The Bible advises to "*set your mind on the things above, not on the things that are on earth.*" (Colossians 3:2)

Listen to the inner guidance with your heart and not your head. Dream dreams that are worthy of you. The mind is like a monkey; it jumps from one object to another. Wise sages of ancient times have therefore advised against listening to the *commands* of an undisciplined mind. Dalai Lama says that *"the undisciplined mind is like an elephant. If left to blunder around out of control, it will wreak havoc."*

Therefore, be sure to listen to your heart and not your mind. Let your actions be inspired by the promptings of the Self. Do not blindly follow the orders of anyone else. Properly discriminate if the path resonates with your heart. If it does not, then do not proceed. These all fall under *"royal commands that should not be obeyed."* Discipline your mind so that it learns to be obedient to serve the very purpose you have set for yourself in life.

Sun Tzu's phrase "nine variations" does not refer to nine actual principles. According to many ancient legends, the number nine is symbolic of infinity. It is found in Chinese mythology that number nine is used to refer to heavenly objects or structures (e.g. the "Ninth Heaven" and "Nine Dragons"). The Indians also revere the number nine as a divine number.

Therefore, the man who knows the eternal wisdom of the Self will know the Truth of his divinity. He will know how to direct his intellect and mind to accomplish his goals. Since he understands how the Universal Law operates, he can use it to fulfil the mission he has set for himself in life.

Regardless of how educated or skilled you may be in a particular field, your ability to excel is limited unless you align yourself with the Universal force. Those who do not know the nature of the mind simply cannot utilise it to their advantage. Man can only reveal his full potential if he knows how to utilise the infallible Universal Law.

是故智者之慮，必雜于利害，雜于利而務可信也，雜于害而患可
解也。是故屈諸侯者以害，役諸侯者以業，趨諸侯者以利。

Therefore, wise are those who examine both advantages and disadvantages in any given situation. Devoting oneself to deliberate on the advantages enables one to determine if the quest is worthy of pursuit. Analysing the disadvantages on the other hand allows one to find solutions for difficulties and adversities. Subdue the feudal lords by showing them potential harm, create trouble for them to keep them constantly engaged and lure them with advantages to hasten them to any location.

Sun Tzu also stresses on the importance of foresight. Make it a constant habit to conduct Self-enquiry. You must carefully analyse both the advantages and disadvantages that follow the fulfilment of your objectives. Deliberate on the purpose of your desire. What goodness will its realisation bring to your life and others'? Listing out the positive effects of the materialisation of your goal reaffirms its worth within yourself. Being clear of your intentions helps build a strong volition to bring the goal into reality.

When you conduct Self-enquiry, you allow yourself to see the error of your ways. This gives you the opportunity to remove them efficiently so that they do not impede your progress in objectifying your goals. Remove any trace of impurity (doubts) from your mind that defies the reality of your vision as soon as it comes to your attention. The process of Self-enquiry reminds you of the end you truly desire and helps calibrate your attention on it. Manoeuvre your way around any problem and continue your journey.

Sun Tzu advises that you should not be enslaved by circumstances. Instead, you should be the one who is in control of it. Be the Master of your mind. You are the only one who decides if a particular mental state should continue or cease to exist in your mind.

故用兵之法，無恃其不來，恃吾有以待之；無恃其不攻，恃吾有所不可攻也。

Therefore, the principles of warfare tell us not to take it for granted that the enemy may not be coming, but to rely on your preparations to be ready for receiving them instead.. Also do not take it for granted that the enemy will not attack, but be prepared in such a way that you cannot be attacked.

To take anything for granted suggests a weak willpower or even laziness. This is the hallmark of foolishness. To not take anything for granted does not mean that you will have to prepare for the possibility of a negative outcome. Doing so will only imprint the negative mental picture on your subconscious mind and subsequently, materialise it in your experience. You should instead ascertain if you have faith in your vision or if you still dwell on expectations. To have expectations is to be doomed to disappointment for there is still room for doubts to exist. Only with faith can one cross the ocean of Samsara (the cycle of life).

Therefore, be always alert. Keep watch for any negative thoughts or emotions that you harbour within. Cultivate faith in you that you allow nothing to shake your confidence in the pursuit of goals that are worthy of you. Face whatever circumstances that come your way boldly. If you have unwavering faith in your vision, you can be assured that nothing can ever keep you away from it.

故將有五危：必死可殺，必生可虜，忿速可侮，廉潔可辱，愛民可煩；凡此五危，將之過也，用兵之災也。覆軍殺將，必以五危，不可不察也。

The General may be faced with five dangers:

1) *Recklessness can cause one to be killed.*
2) *Cowardice allows one to be captured.*
3) *He who is quick-tempered can be easily provoked.*
4) *He who is pure and upright in character can fall prey to shame.*
5) *He who is attached to his subjects can cause him frustration.*

These are the five dangerous traps that a General must not fall into for they are disastrous to one's leadership. The fault definitely lies among these five traps for an army that is overthrown with their General killed. They must therefore be meditated upon.

There are five dangerous traps that man can fall into during his journey of manifesting his ideals. For those whose ideals do not materialise or who lead an unfulfilled life, *the fault definitely lies among these five traps*:

1) Recklessness:
Acting out of impulse will always land you in trouble. It is crucial that man examines the pros and cons when he sets himself a mission. Carelessness in managing his thoughts and feelings does not only cause his vision to not materialise, but also *kills* his enthusiasm in continuing the journey to bring it into reality.

Unaware that the fault lies in the defect of his technique, man's willpower becomes weakened after several failed attempts to manifest his goals. He eventually becomes discouraged from setting any big objective that he deems 'unrealistic' in life.

Therefore, it is crucial that man manoeuvres his thoughts and feelings in the right direction; to dwell only on the mental states that he wishes to objectify on the physical plane and not allow his mind to wander as it pleases.

2) Cowardice:

Fear will only do you more harm than good. You can never move forward in life if you allow fear to dominate your mind; it stagnates your development. Chinese philosopher Lao-Tzu says that "*the journey of a thousand miles begins with one single step.*"

Therefore, do not let what you deem "unrealistic" hinder your progress. All successful-minded people share a similar trait; they all believe in an ideal that is so different from the rest of the world. That is why Will Smith says that "*being realistic is (actually) the most commonly travelled road to mediocrity.*" So, think out of the box and believe in your vision.

There is a story of how Thomas Edison failed thousands of times when trying to create the light bulb. Before he successfully invented it, no one has even heard of such a thing! Who would have thought that his objective was a realistic one? Nonetheless, he still persevered in his vision and at the end of the day, it just had to be a concrete fact on this objective plane. What was more interesting is that Thomas Edison never saw that he had 'failed' thousands of times. Instead, he said that he had successfully discovered thousands of ways how **not** to make a light bulb! This is the positive fighting spirit that all should live by. Do not be afraid to make mistakes. Acknowledging and learning from every mistake is a step towards perfection.

Therefore, be bold and dare to dream! Move forward, one step at a time. Regardless of how small the step is, just remember to keep moving. Do not worry about the possibility of failure. You have more to lose if you do not even try. If all the great scientists of the past allowed their fears to conquer their soul, you would not be enjoying the comforts that you do today such as electricity, telephone, cars, aircrafts and more.

3) Temper:

To be *quick-tempered* is the worst quality that man can have for it leads him to hasty decisions. You can be easily *provoked* if you are quick-tempered. Just mere words are enough to aggravate your fire and cause you to be restless. Why give others the power to control your mind? The man who is quick-tempered often loses focus on his actual goal. Harbouring anger within will only replicate similar circumstances to recur in the future.

4) Seeking for approval:

Generally, most people do crave for society's approval in all they do whether it is behaviour, fashion, beliefs or others. This is a dangerous trap as those who desire for public approval will easily fall prey to *shame*. They wish to be accepted and seen by the rest of society as an obedient individual who lives up to the expectations already set by others.

It will be difficult for such individuals to ever come up with something new for they prefer to follow the herd. Because they are very particular about what others think of them, they have transferred the power to society's hands to sketch their lives on their behalf.

If you happen to fall into this category, the question to ask yourself is: *Why do you try to fit in when you can stand out?* It is unimportant if others think your goal is realistic or unrealistic. What is important however, is what you yourself actually think about it!

It is alright to be unique. Just because others think that a particular goal is unattainable does not make it so. People laughed at Alexander Graham Bell when he believed that he could invent something called a "telephone" that will be used in every home. Had he been the type to seek for society's approval, there would be no telephones or mobile phones today.

Success lies in being unique. If you do the things that the rest are doing, you will only get the same results that they are getting. Therefore, define yourself. Do not let others have the power over you to determine what you are capable of!

5) *Attachment:*

Attachment is the source of man's misery. Being attached to your desires, you are still holding onto the feelings of "want" and thus, you remain dissatisfied that they have not been fulfilled. Your current experience cannot change unless you move from dwelling in the mental state of "want" to "already is".

So, one of the biggest mistakes that Mental Science students commit is to hold onto their desires too tightly when attempting to manifest their ideals. This is the cause of their *frustration* when their ideals do not materialise. The Universal Law states that what is without is from within. So, if you find yourself still desiring for that thing, you accept the fact in your own mind that the need has still not been fulfilled, and therefore, it must be so!

Swami Vivekananda says that *"almost all our suffering is caused by our not having the power of detachment. So along with the development of concentration, we must develop the power of detachment."*

If you have faith that your vision is already true to your circumstances, you will no longer be *attached* to the feeling of wanting it since it already is and it will soon become your reality.

9 - 行軍

THE MARCH

孫子曰：凡處軍相敵：絕山依谷，視生處高，戰隆無登，此處山之軍也。

Sun Tzu said: Generally, the rules to position an army and facing the enemy are as follow: the army is to stay close to the valleys when crossing mountains, camp on high grounds for survival and during intense battle, the army is to fight downhill. This is how we organise the army in the mountains.

This chapter lists the rules for man to follow in order to manifest his ideals and to overcome the challenges that he may face during the journey.

Obstacles are a part of life. They will only impede your way if you allow them to. In fact, they do not exist at all in the mind of the successful man. Obstacles only appear to be what they are when you take your eyes off your actual goal.

Success is not measured by one's status in society but by the obstacles that one has successfully overcome. The ups and downs you experience in life are the colours of your story. See all obstacles as stepping stones to build the life you want.

Frank A. Clark once said that *"if you can find a path with no obstacles, it probably doesn't lead anywhere."*

We are expanding every single day. The problem that you once thought was as huge as a *mountain* is no longer a threat to the current 'you' because you have found ways to overcome it. This problem has since then faded into the background of your life.

So, do not be disheartened when you find obstacles in your way. An obstacle is often an unrecognised opportunity. Figure out a way to work around it. Just like how an army can circumvent a *mountain* by passing through a *valley*, you can also find ways to work around the obstacles that lie before you. Where there is a will, there is always a way.

"History has demonstrated that the most notable winners usually encountered heartbreaking obstacles before they triumphed. They won because they refused to become discouraged by their defeats." (B.C. Forbes)

Sun Tzu advises the army to *"camp on high grounds for survival"*. This is also relatively true for those who would like to solve a problem. The best thing to do is to step out of the box. Problems often appear overwhelming because you see yourself as the victim. By doing so, you are drowning yourself in misery. However, if you step out and look at your problems from the view of a neutral third party, you may discover that they are not so big after all. Therefore, the key here is to always be positive and to not entangle your mind with the obstacles that you encounter in your path. Clarity of vision will definitely help you find the solutions to your problems.

絕水必遠水，客絕水而來，勿迎于水內，令半濟而擊之利。欲戰者，無附于水而迎客，視生處高，無迎水流，此處水上之軍也。

One must be very careful to distance oneself from the water when crossing a river. When invaders cross the river, do not meet them in the water. Instead, allow half of their force to cross over before taking the advantage to attack them. Those who desire battle should not face the enemy near the waters. Observe all movements from higher ground but do not meet them in the water. This is how we organise the army near the waters.

When you *cross the river* of life, also known as the ocean of Samsara (suffering), do not be afflicted by the variety of circumstances that may drown you. Although it is inevitable that one needs to cross this river, *distance yourself from the water*.

Throughout your journey, you are bound to meet people who will challenge your decisions, beliefs and ways of life. Drowned by their limited ideas, they will entice you to join them *in the water* (of suffering). After all, the world exists on a collective consensus and anyone who does not conform to its established rules is looked upon as the enemy. The role of the Self is that of a passive observer. You can *observe* everything that takes place in this Universe, but remember never to be attached to them.

The Bible advises that man can be in the world, but not of the world. So, be still. Do not react to criticisms or give in to the persuasion by others to follow their limited ways. You do not need to tread down the path that others have laid when you can build your very own.

"Never argue with stupid people, they will drag you down to their level and then beat you with experience." (Mark Twain)

絕斥澤，惟亟去勿留，若交軍于斥澤之中，必依水草，而背眾樹，此處斥澤之軍也。

Cross wetlands quickly. Do not linger around the area. If an army is required to do battle in wetlands, the soldiers must stay near the grass with their backs against the trees. This is how we organise the army on wetlands.

Treading on *wetlands* is symbolic of dwelling on uncertainties. Sun Tzu advises you not to *linger around* for too long because it makes you vulnerable. To be successful in life, you will need to stand on solid ground. Set yourself a purpose and fight for it. Stand strongly on your goals and even the sky will not be your limit. If you do not make up your mind, you can be sure that you will sink with each passing second as time is continuously ticking and can never be rewound.

Whenever you are indecisive with the options available around you, constantly remind yourself of the final goal. Just as how the *grass* can help rescue sinking *soldiers* in the wetlands, remembering where you want to end up in life will also save you from giving up on your dream during turbulent times. Guide your actions according to the outcome you desire to experience.

To have your *"back against the tree"* is to know with absolute certainty of what you would like to achieve in life. Being precise in your mind confers you great strength to overcome the challenges you may face in your journey towards realising your goal.

平陸處易，右背高，前死後生，此處平陸之軍也。

On levelled-ground, position the army in a way that it is easy for them to manoeuvre their movements. They should be supported by high ground on the right. The army should be facing dangerous grounds with their backs against safety. This is how we organise the army on levelled-ground.

When you come face-to-face with people who challenge your views and beliefs, do not feel threatened or confined by their judgments. You do not become stupid simply because others say that you are. Take control of the situation by remaining calm and direct your inner senses to 'see' and 'hear' only that which pleases you.

Sun Tzu also mentions that the army *"should be supported by high ground on the right"*. The right side of the brain is usually linked to creativity. Interpreted fourth-dimensionally, this paragraph therefore calls for man to support his efforts to attain his ideals by relying on the creative faculty of the mind.

The fault of an unfulfilled dream does not lie with circumstances or the people whom you meet along the way, but with a defective inner vision. Nothing can impede you from reaching your goal unless you allow it to. Therefore, face opposing forces (*dangerous grounds*) courageously, knowing that you alone hold the key to your destiny (*back against safety*). This is the technique to confront your adversaries.

凡此四軍之利，黃帝之所以勝四帝也。

These are the four general advantages an army can employ that had helped the Yellow emperor to gain victory over other four rulers.

The Yellow emperor had gained victory over other four rulers by adhering to these four general rules. You too can benefit from these principles and be victorious in your journey towards success if you apply them properly.

凡軍好高而惡下，貴陽而賤陰，養生處實，軍無百疾，是謂必勝。

Generally, all armies prefer high grounds to lower ones. They appreciate brightness but have an aversion for darkness. The men sustain their health with a disciplined routine so that they are not afflicted with all kinds of diseases. These factors ascertain victory if they are fulfilled.

All beings aspire for a higher realm of existence. Everyone in this world feels good whenever they are happy. If only people knew that the choice of happiness lies with them, they would definitely choose to be happy.

"When I was five years old, my mother always told me that happiness was the key to life. When I went to school, they asked me what I wanted to be when I grew up. I wrote down 'happy'. They told me that I did not understand the assignment and I told them that they did not understand life." (John Lennon)

Happiness is not a destination. It is the way of life and the means to bring you to the destination that you have set for yourself. There is no need to crave for happiness. When you allow yourself to be contented with the perfection of all there is, you will be happy. Vedic scriptures state that man's nature is verily *"Ananda"* (bliss). Therefore, allow yourself to just be.

"Happiness is like a butterfly; the more you chase it, the more it will elude you. But if you turn your attention to other things, it will come and sit softly on your shoulder." (Henry David Thoreau)

To consciously allow yourself to be happy will also confer you good health. It is sheer ignorance to think that man's mood does not affect his body. In fact, every thought affects every single cell of the body. The cycle also applies the other way round; one is happy when the body is *not afflicted with all kinds of diseases.*

Health is wealth. Only when man is healthy can he fully concentrate on his goals. This is why it is so important for him to *sustain (his) health with a disciplined routine.* A disciplined routine does not only ensure optimum health, but also increases your willpower in getting things done the way you want them to.

邱陵隄防，必處其陽，而右背之，此兵之利，地之助也。上雨水沫至，欲涉者，待其定也。

As a protection measure in the hills and embankments, the army must be positioned where it is bright with their right side supported with the slope. This positioning benefits the army by utilising the natural advantages that the ground has to offer. For those who wish to wade across the river whose current is strong due to rain upstream should wait until it settles first.

Already mentioned earlier in this chapter, it is important for one to possess a positive mental attitude in order to protect one's dream when facing the obstacles that life present us with. Do not see undesirable circumstances as they are but start 'seeing' them like you want them to be. Always remember to keep your attention on the *bright* side and rely on your creative faculties to work towards your dream.

Majority of the people have the tendency to think that their life would have been easier if only they did not lack certain resources. However, man has already been endowed with everything that he ever needs – willpower. As the Bible states, *"God will never give you more than you can handle"*. Man's circumstances need not be different in order for him to live the life he desires. All he has to do is to make the most out of all his resources to work towards his vision.

Whenever you experience a turbulent situation (*river whose current is strong*), do not react. Reacting to it will only further affirm its existence in your subconscious mind, which will subsequently produce more of such similar situation in your experience. Time is a great healer. So, whenever you find yourself stressed out with your situation, calm down and be patient. There is always light at the end of the tunnel. You will see that this restless phase shall end soon. Once the situation begins to *settle*, plan and then act from there.

"Patience is not passive; on the contrary, it is concentrated strength."
(Bruce Lee)

凡地有絕澗、天井、天牢、天羅、天陷、天隙，必亟去之，勿近也；吾遠之，敵近之；吾迎之，敵背之。

The army is advised not to go near dangerous ravines, deep natural hollows, confined spaces, natural entangling thickets, natural pits and crevasses. They are to quickly march away from such settings. Although we should avoid these places, draw the enemy to approach them; while we face them, the enemy should have their backs against such settings.

Do not subject yourself to limits. If you begin to notice your mind getting *entangled* in the psychological trap of negativity, *"quickly march away"* from it. Draw your mind back to focusing on the end result that you desire to experience.

Ensure that you invest your assets (be it material, physical or psychological) wisely. Just as an army that possesses great strength can invite unnecessary challenges by going near *"dangerous ravines, deep natural hollows, confined spaces, natural entangling thickets, natural pits and crevasses"*, man's capacity to live his life to his maximum potential is undermined when he allows his mind to dwell on negative thoughts.

Interpreted fourth-dimensionally, *"the enemy (who) have their backs against such settings"* simply means that any undesirable circumstances are sustained by negative thoughts, which is *dangerous* for your journey to fulfil your goals.

軍旁有險阻、潢井、蒹葭、林木、翳薈者，必謹覆索之，此伏姦
之所也。

Should the army be surrounded with hills, ponds, pits, tall reeds or a forest, search the area carefully and thoroughly as these are ideal places where the enemy may lie in ambush.

Evil lurks in the back of your mind, which is ready to pounce on you as soon as you let your guard down.

The mind is akin to a mad monkey. Its attention constantly moves from one object to another. Hence, never leave your mind idle. Otherwise, it will begin to reach out to fanciful thoughts that may not serve you or others well. For example, allowing the mind to idle on thoughts of war will only instil fear within your consciousness and manifest more wars in the physical world. That is why it is important for one to be selective over the things that one pays attention to. This includes (but not limited to) the content that one reads in books or newspapers and the type of dramas that one watches on television. If you truly want to change your life, you must be prepared to first change your habits.

Always mind the mind. Be ever watchful of the ideas that you assimilate from your external surroundings. Knowing now that everything in the world is yourself pushed out, you would want to discipline yourself to retain only constructive thoughts and weed out destructive ones from the garden of your mind.

It is either you learn to transcend the mind to experience the no-thought state, or engage your mind to dwell only on constructive thoughts that will bring you closer to desirable ideals. Therefore, only give your attention to lovely ideas that you would like to experience in your world and ignore those that you would not like to see materialised. Otherwise, undesirable experiences await you "*in ambush*".

敵近而靜者，恃其險也。遠而挑戰者，欲人之進也。其所居易者，利也。

An enemy nearby that remains quiet is relying on his natural strength of his position. The enemy who is far away but challenges you to a battle will attempt to provoke you to advance to their location as he may be occupying a location that is to his advantage.

During war, the army does not blindly react to any situation. The wise General is to decipher the intention behind the enemy's actions.

Similarly, not everything that you hear from others is true or worthy of you. Just because someone calls you a fool does not make you one! Carefully examine the motive behind other people's actions and words to conclude if they should be taken seriously. There is a possibility that some will attempt to discourage you from achieving the success that you deserve simply because they do not have the confidence to join you. Observing your success puts too much pressure on them to question their own value. Too afraid to change their ways, it is easier for them to entice you to stay exactly where they are – in their comfort zone. This is the reason why Woodrow T. Wilson says that "*if you want to make enemies, try to change something.*"

So, do not be fooled by appearances. Do not let anyone else hold the pen when writing the story of your life.

眾樹動者，來也。眾草多障者，疑也。鳥起者，伏也。獸駭者，覆也。

Movement of trees indicates that the enemy is approaching. Obstructions placed amidst the grass by the enemy are to lead us to be suspicious of their motives. When birds take flight, it means that that the enemy is lying in ambush nearby. If there are signs that the animals are startled, you will know that the enemy is planning to attack.

Everything that exists in this world has a cause and effect. This is known in spirituality as the Law of Causation. When conditions change, the substances produced change and take another form. For example, when water is heated with high temperature as a condition, it evaporates. When vapour comes in contact with cold air as a condition, it condenses and forms a cloud. This change phenomenon also applies to the functions of the mind. There is nothing in this Universe that does not follow this basic rule. As you sow, so shall you reap.

Therefore, to determine if you are headed towards the right direction, engage in the process of introspection. How do you feel about reaching the goals that you have set for yourself? Are you confident that you will make it?

Assess your actions and experiences. They will reveal to you the quality of thoughts that you keep within. If you do not like what you see in your life, change the ideas you hold onto in your mind and your circumstances will also begin to change to reflect the new thought-pattern.

塵：高而銳者，車來也；卑而廣者，徒來也；散而條達者，樵採也；少而往來者，營軍也。

When dust rises high above the ground intensely, this indicates that chariots are approaching. If dust remains low on the ground but spread over a wide area, it is a sign that infantry is approaching. If it is scattered all over the place, you will know that the enemy is gathering firewood. Very little dust flying around signifies that the enemy is encamping.

"Dust" is defined as fine, dry particles of matter. It is very difficult to see dust particles with the naked eye. A sharp vision is necessary for one to be able to detect the movement of *dust* in the air. Likewise, Sun Tzu asks you to develop a sharp inner vision so that you rely more on what you experience within than what you see without.

辭卑而益備者，進也。辭強而進驅者，退也。輕車先出其側者，陣也。無約而請和者，謀也。奔走而陳兵者，期也。半進半退者，誘也。

The enemy who speaks humbly and increases the intensity of preparations are planning an advance. An enemy who utters strong words and advance aggressively are signs of retreat. If the enemy puts out light chariots first to rest by the sides, he is deploying his troops. When the enemy proposes peace between both parties without a treaty, he is strategising. If the enemy rushes to raise his troops, it means that the time he has set for the battle is already drawing near. When the enemy deploys only half of his troops while the other half retreats, he is luring you back to camp.

In this paragraph, one is reminded again not to be fooled by appearances. Things that appear without are not always what they seem to be. The person who speaks obligingly may not always be a friend, and one who seems to contribute to the difficulties in your path also need not necessarily be a foe.

仗而立者，飢也。汲而先飲者，渴也。見利而不進者，勞也。

If the enemy sets aside their weapons, they are hungry. If soldiers who are sent to draw water from the well drink the water first before returning to camp, we will know that the army has inadequate water supply and is suffering from thirst. Soldiers who do not advance to secure an advantage show that they are struggling.

Sun Tzu reminds all that even the enemy is merely human and also has their own problems. Hence, see them not as people who oppose you but develop the compassion to understand the reasons behind their actions.

One's actions tell a lot about their situation. They who discourage you from pursuing your dreams are most likely suffering from their own insecurities. People get angry when they feel that their position is threatened. Those who are outwardly cynical about your enthusiasm to achieve your goals could have also been disappointed in the past when they pursued theirs. The possibilities for people's reactions are endless and so, it is best to not personalise other people's words because the things that they say are only a reflection of the ideas they have been brought up with.

鳥集者，虛也。夜呼者，恐也。軍擾者，將不重也。旌旗動者，亂也。吏怒者，倦也。殺馬肉食者，軍無糧也。懸缶不返其舍者，窮寇也。諄諄翕翕，徐與人言者，失眾也。數賞者，窘也。數罰者，困也。

When birds gather on any spot, it means that the location is unoccupied. Troops that cry during the night are afraid. Disorder amongst troops indicates that the General's authority is weak. If the enemy's flags and pennants are constantly moved about, this indicates that their army is confused. If the officers are easily irritated, this is a sign of exhaustion. Those who start killing horses to feed on their meat imply shortage of provision. The army that hangs up their pottery and does not return to camp shows desperation. If a leader has to repeat his commands and speak obligingly to his men, you will know that the leader has lost their trust. Those who are calculative of bestowing rewards are at great distress. They who punish frequently are facing difficulties in managing the army.

Sun Tzu's use of the term "*night*" in this paragraph symbolises ignorance (darkness). Enveloped by darkness, man becomes a victim to fear. It is due to ignorance that man does not know that he is verily the Master of his mind. You will know that you have not exercised enough *authority* over your mind when your thoughts, words and deeds are not congruent. One-pointedness is the only way to consciously will your dream to come into being. Below are few of the common characteristics that people with an undisciplined mind share:

If you keep changing your goals, you demonstrate that you do not really know what you actually want. You have not yet ascertained the destination that you would like to move towards. Staying *confused* will not bring you anywhere.

"The number one reason most people do not get what they want is that they do not know what they want. Clarity is power. Rich people do not send mixed messages to the universe; poor people do." (T. Harv Eker)

So, set yourself a goal, however small it may be, and work your way towards it (at least for now). Once you have successfully achieved this small step, you will be ready for bigger ones.

If you find yourself easily *irritated* with life, this shows that your life is stagnant. You are *exhausted* because you seem to be going nowhere. One who leads a fulfilled life is one who has a vision that they can place their heart and soul into. A life void of dreams is meaningless.

Not only must you set objectives for yourself, you must also work towards them. People often say that they want change and they would like to lead the life they dream about, but when you observe their actions, they do nothing that will contribute to the materialisation of these dreams. If you want something different than what you already have now, you have to start doing something different than what you are doing now!

Horses are extremely important during ancient battles. These animals made it possible for the army to travel long distances to conquer their adversaries. Interpreted fourth-dimensionally, to *"(kill) horses to feed on their meat (due to) shortage of provision"* is akin to man killing his dream as a result of a weak willpower to withstand the journey to materialise it. Being so negatively oriented, any opportunity that comes his way is often overlooked.

Pottery on the other hand is used to cook food to rejuvenate the army's strength. *The army that hangs up their pottery* shows that they have given up hope in fighting the battle. This also applies to individuals who have given up hope in their dreams. Not having faith in the Universal Law, they become *desperate* and impatient. Consequently after a short while not seeing any result from their actions, they just leave their dreams to wilt and die.

If you still see any situation as it is instead of 'seeing' it the way you want it to be, then you are still enslaved by your five physical senses. When you react negatively to circumstances, it shows that you have no faith in the Self where infinite power is. Those who are critical of themselves *are at great distress* as they only see themselves as beings that are full of faults instead of an infinite being that is capable of achieving anything that they set their mind to. They who constantly chide themselves clearly have not yet mastered the mind and thus *face difficulties* in moving toward the life that they desire.

先暴而後畏其眾者，不精之至也。來委謝者，欲休息也。兵怒而相迎，久而不合，又不相去，必謹察之。

Those who first behave violently and only later fear the multitude of the enemy's army lacks proficiency. When offerings are sent, the enemy desires truce. If the enemy's troops confront you with anger but remains at the same position for a long time without either engaging in battle or leaving the place, one must carefully investigate the reason for this.

Man's ignorance is further exemplified when he tries to fight against negative thoughts and circumstances only to realise later that the more he pushes against them, the more power they have over him.

What you push against always pushes against you. Harshly reprimanding yourself for thinking negative thoughts will only imprint them more strongly on your subconscious mind.

Everything without is actually within. Knowing now that the mistake lies with a negative thought-pattern in your mind that had contributed to this problem, you would have then declared *truce* with that undesirable situation. Having discovered the mistake, you now have the power to correct the idea to form a different end result.

Therefore, when you are faced with an unlovely situation, do not jump the gun and react to it. Carefully *investigate* the source of the problem and contemplate on the possible ways that you can overcome it with. There is always a reason behind each experience. Examine the faults of your own inner vision that had caused such an unlovely experience to materialise. Learn from it, correct it and never repeat it again.

兵非貴益多，惟無武進，足以併力料敵取人而已。夫惟無慮而易敵者，必擒于人。

Possessing a large army need not necessarily be an advantage in warfare. It only hinders the enemy from coming near one's territory. It is enough for an army to combine all available forces, speculate the enemy's next move and then only attack him. He who lacks foresight and underestimates his enemy will surely be captured.

Just because you have plenty of resources to help bring your dreams into being does not mean that you have the *advantage* to continue succeeding. No matter how high you have climbed up the ladder of success, it does not indicate that you have completely conquered your mind. It only gives people less reasons to tell you why you 'cannot' achieve something because majority of the people only trust what they can already see around them.

The son of a millionaire can still lose his inheritance the next day if he does not know how to exercise his mind to work towards his goal. Most of the successful figures in this world today did not come from wealthy families. Their success is owed to hard work and confidence in their dreams. So, even if you were to start with nothing at all, so long you make the best use of all of your resources and protect yourself from falling prey to the *enemy* of doubt, fear and anxiety, you can still succeed.

Life is like a game of Scrabble. Though you do not know what letters you will get from the box (and you cannot choose), you will do your best to re-arrange the seven letters to score the highest points possible. Similarly, you may not always know what life is going to hand over to you. All you can do is to make the best of what you do have to live the best life you can.

They who *lack foresight* and *underestimate* the *enemy* take it for granted that it is not important to keep watch on their mental activities. They cannot see how crucial it is to weed negative thoughts from the mind that will materialise on this physical plane over time. Such ignorance will surely make them victims to negative circumstances, thus resulting in suffering and misery.

卒未親附而罰之，則不服，不服則難用。卒已親附而罰不行，則不可用。故令之以文，齊之以武，是謂必取。

If one were to punish the army before a bond of loyalty is formed, the soldiers will rebel. When they are rebellious, this makes them practically useless to the entire force. Similarly, even if the soldiers have already formed a very close bond to the commander that makes it impossible for one to punish them, this also renders them useless to the force. Therefore, command and lead the army with compassion but unite them by exercising discipline. This is the definite way of conquering the hearts of your men.

Not knowing how to keep your mind and senses under control so that they follow orders from the Self to focus only on the ideals that you want to manifest in life will result in chaos. Constantly criticising yourself for the mistakes that you have done in the past will only attract more similar episodes as you give your undivided attention to them. Fuelled with anger towards yourself, you allow the mistakes of the past to step on your head, rendering you a useless warrior in the journey of mind mastery. While it is important to be strict with yourself so as not to repeat these mistakes, handle them with compassion and understand that *"to err is human, but to forgive is divine."*

What most do however is to follow wherever their monkey mind brings them. This habit stems from ignorance as the people do not know the benefits that they can reap from a disciplined mind. Not controlling the mind as the Master, it cannot be fully utilised to achieve their goals in life. Therefore, it is important to ensure that the hierarchy of power is properly maintained. Remember that the Master is the Self and not the mind. Master your mind and *conquer* your life.

令素行以教其民，則民服；令不素行以教其民，則民不服；令素行，與眾相得也。

Enforcing discipline consistently on all men will ensure obedience. On the other hand, should disciplinary actions be enforced inconsistently amongst the men, the force is bound to retaliate. When one enforces a consistent pattern within the army, the benefits to be reaped are mutual.

Equanimity is the hallmark of the man who has mastered his mind. It is a state of stability or composure arising from a deep awareness and acceptance of the present moment. One should not be elated by pleasure and be depressed by pain.

Sri Sathya Sai Baba says that "*anything that helps you maintain unruffled equanimity is right action.*"

Treat both good and bad situations alike. Rise above duality. Be unmoved by your circumstances. Remain convicted in the vision that you 'see' within. Know that your life experiences are merely the result of the ideas that your mind dwell upon. Should any undesirable situation arises, know that every adversity is a seed of greater benefit. Train your mind to 'see' only goodness in everything.

With faith in your vision, you will treat everything that comes your way with equanimity. Your mind is already geared to materialise that particular objective that you have set for yourself and you will allow nothing to stop you.

10 - 地形
TERRAIN

孫子曰：地形有通者，有挂者，有支者，有隘者，有險者，有遠者。

Sun Tzu said: There are different types of terrains:

1) *Open ground*
2) *Entangling ground*
3) *Stalemate ground*
4) *Narrow ground*
5) *Dangerous ground*
6) *Distant ground*

This chapter introduces the few types of possible situations that man can expect to encounter at certain stages of his life and what he must do to manage them. The scope of situations that he can encounter is so wide that it is impossible to list all of them.

我可以往，彼可以來，曰通；通形者，先居高陽，利糧道以戰，則利。

An open ground is one that both we and the enemy can freely traverse through; be the first to occupy the favourable spot (high and sunny side) to benefit from a good route of supply, which is advantageous for one during a battle.

Applying a fourth-dimensional interpretation of an "*open ground*", it can be seen as a situation whereby one is not subjected to any restriction to set their goals.

To occupy the "*high and sunny side*" is to dream dreams that nourish your soul. Success is usually borne out of passion. Setting your mind on doing the things you love will give you the strength to endure the journey to materialise them.

Stressing on the importance of passion, German philosopher Georg Wilhelm Friedrich Hegel says that "*nothing great in the world has ever been accomplished without passion.*"

So, do all the things that will keep your spirit *high*. These can include reading, listening to music, meditating, exercising or any other activity that will boost your mood and empower you. This is how you "*benefit from a good route of (spiritual) supply*", which will help you achieve your goals.

"There is no passion to be found in playing small — in settling for a life that is less than the one you are capable of living." (Nelson Mandela)

可以往，難以返，曰挂；挂形者，敵無備，出而勝之，敵若有備，出而不勝，難以返，不利。

An entangling ground is one that can be entered but will be difficult to exit; in such a ground, victory can be gained if one enters and strike the enemy that is unprepared. However, if one strikes an enemy that is prepared and does not succeed, one's position becomes unfavourable as the army finds it difficult to withdraw.

This paragraph refers to stepping into situations that bind you. Examples of such situations can include (but not limited to) contractual agreements and marriage. You are therefore advised to exercise discretion before committing yourself into these situations. Go ahead only if you have the confidence that you can manage it and fulfil the requirements that are expected of you. Otherwise, you may be inviting trouble and it will be difficult for you to *withdraw*.

Here, Sun Tzu is suggesting that one must accept responsibility over his or her decisions regardless of the outcome. Owning up to your mistakes is in fact, the first step towards self-empowerment as you reaffirm to yourself that you are the one who is solely in control of your life instead of other people.

我出而不利，彼出而不利，曰支；支形者，敵雖利我，我無出也；引而去之，令敵半出而擊之，利。

One is on stalemate ground when neither army has an advantage to strike first. On such ground, do not make the first move even if the enemy tries to lure you with an advantage. Withdraw the army and leave the place. This will in turn lure the enemy to make a move first instead. Once half of their troops have advanced towards you, it is then advantageous to strike.

One is on *"stalemate ground"* when he or she has no idea what they would like to achieve in life. Since there is no set purpose, you are not moving in any particular direction.

When the mind is idle, it gives negative thoughts the opportunity to occupy it. Even if an idea that does not resonate with your heart appears tempting, do not entertain it. Choose the path that makes your heart sing. The world may try to convince you by listing out the advantages that you can receive by following its already established ways, but if it is not what you truly want, you are not going to be happy!

Seeing you unmoved by temptations and the height of faith that you possess in your dream, the world will eventually have to make way for its realisation for Neville Goddard says that *"an assumption, though false, will become a fact if persisted."* When the opportunity to manifest your dream is presented to you, it is then the right time to act.

隘形者，我先居之，必盈以待敵；若敵先居之，盈而勿從，不盈而從之。

On a narrow ground, be the first to occupy the space and fill the area with your own men while you wait for the enemy to arrive. If however the enemy reaches first, do not attack them if the area is strongly garrisoned. Attack them only if the area is weakly garrisoned.

A *"narrow ground"* is similar to an *"entrapping ground"*. They both suggest situations that involve risk.

"Only those who will risk going too far can possibly find out how far one can go." (T.S. Eliott)

You will have to analyse your situation carefully to determine if you are ready to take it on. If you are mentally prepared to face the possible challenges that may come your way by walking down that path, then proceed.

Andre Malraux says that *"often the difference between a successful person and a failure is not one has better abilities or ideas, but the courage that one has to bet on one's ideas, to take a calculated risk and to act."*

However, when you find yourself hesitating on taking the next step, it shows that you have traces of negativity in your mind. If you allow fear to dominate your consciousness, you would have already lost the battle even before it actually begins. When you fear, you emit negative thought-patterns that draw more challenges than the situation normally would, thus heightening the risk level. Failure is inevitable for those who dwell on fear. Unless you can conquer fear and be prepared to weather through storm and sunshine, it is best that you do not enter into such situations.

險形者，我先居之，必居高陽以待敵；若敵先居之，引而去之，勿從也。

If one is the first to occupy a space on dangerous grounds, then it is crucial that one positions oneself on high ground to wait for the enemy. If the enemy occupies the area first, do not battle with them. Withdraw the army and leave.

An army on "*dangerous grounds*" is required to be swift and quick-witted when making decisions. This paragraph suggests that one must know how to prioritise. In all situations, do not waste your time and energy on petty matters. Instead, decide what is important for you and then pursue it. To "*position (yourself) on high ground*" means you must consider all aspects of the situation carefully before coming to a decision.

遠形者，勢均，難以挑戰，戰而不利。

If both armies with equal strength are separated by a great distance, it will be difficult to challenge the enemy. It is unfavourable for one to fight a battle on such ground.

This paragraph implies that one must take a stand in life. The nature of the mind is such that when you direct your mind to focus on something, it cannot possibly focus on another. When you choose to adopt a positive mental attitude in your endeavours, you cannot possibly be dwelling on negativity as well (*separated by great distance*). Not taking a stand to either be positive or negative in one's approach is to allow both to have *equal strength*. To waddle through life with uncertainty is to be doomed to mediocrity. Only when man sets a purpose for himself can he fight and win the battle of life!

凡此六者，地之道也，將之至任，不可不察也。

As these are the six main principles of exploiting the different types of terrains, it is therefore every General's responsibility to examine them.

Above are the *six main principles* of managing the different situations that you may encounter in life. It is therefore important for anyone who wants to be the Mastermind of their life to *examine them*.

故兵有走者，有弛者，有陷者，有崩者，有亂者，有北者；凡此六者，非天地之災，將之過也。

The military experiences various problems such as runaways, insubordination, falling, collapse, chaos and defeat. These six problems do not arise from natural causes but from the faults of the General.

Throughout the journey of your life, there will be times when you will:

a)   Ignore opportunities that may come your way (*runaways*);

b) Experience that your mind does not follow the orders from the Self to focus only on the goals that you would like to manifest in your experience (*insubordination*);

c) Feel discouraged from working towards your goals (*falling*);

d) Make bad decisions that bring undesirable circumstances (*collapse*);

e) Be trapped in difficult situations that appear as though there is no way out (*chaos*); and,

f) Give up on your goals (*defeat*).

These are not problems that are influenced by your circumstances (*natural causes*) but are faults of your very own mind (*the General*).

夫勢均，以一擊十，曰走。

With both forces being equal, using one to attack ten will result the former to be intimidated and therefore run away.

One has *equal* chances of allowing positivity or negativity to dominate the consciousness. Allowing negative thoughts to imbue your mind in regards to any matter will eventually allow them to overpower you. It will be difficult for you to instil any positive thought as you shudder at the idea of failure. You may then not even attempt to pursue the goal that you had in mind as you will be intimidated by it and thus *run away* from it.

卒強吏弱，曰弛。吏強卒弱，曰陷。大吏怒而不服，遇敵懟而自戰，將不知其能，曰崩。

If the soldiers are stronger than their officers, insubordination will arise. When the officers are too strong while the soldiers are too weak, the army will still fall. A high-ranking officer whom, out of hate, gets angry, rebels and declares war against the enemy without first seeking counsel from the General to know if the army is ready for battle not only causes a collapse in the system, but also leads the army to ruin.

The key here is to work in harmony. Sun Tzu suggests that if you allow the mind that is supposed to be under your control to run free without discipline, *insubordination will arise.* The mind will begin to attach itself to ideas that are of no value to you and manifest them in your life experience. Insufficient discipline exercised on the mind also leads you to act out of impulse, which is a dangerous trait and is borne out of ignorance. Thus, instead of you assuming your rightful role as the Master of your mind, you would have allowed the monkey mind to be the master of your fate.

Nothing is impossible for those who operate in the divine consciousness. The Self is all-powerful. It is only when you know how to align the Self, intellect, mind and senses to work together towards a particular goal that you can be the Master of your life.

將弱不嚴，教道不明，吏卒無常，陳兵縱橫，曰亂。

A General, who is weak and not strict, whose teachings and directions are also unclear, his officers and soldiers will lack discipline and the organisation of the army becomes haphazard. This will lead to chaos.

It is important to create a vivid image in your mind of a wish fulfilled to impress it upon your subconscious mind in order to manifest it. The importance of being clear about what you want to experience in life cannot be stressed enough. Vague ideas equal vague results. Once you have identified the ideal that you would like to materialise in your experience, stick to it with unwavering faith.

The value of having confidence in your vision can be illustrated using an example of a visit to a restaurant. If you have ordered spinach pie, you will need to have faith that the waiter who has taken your order will notify the chef about your selection, and then wait for the chef to prepare the meal. If you were to change your order every few minutes, you clearly do not know what you would like to have on your plate. Eventually, the restaurant personnel will not take your orders seriously and you will end up having nothing to eat.

Similarly, if what you want is to experience financial freedom, you need to send out a clear image to the subconscious mind to manifest it for you. Imagine vividly in your mind a scene that suggests financial freedom and you are sure to experience it in good time. If however you believe that that state is yours today but doubt its truth tomorrow, you are sending *unclear directions* to the subconscious mind. Everything then becomes *haphazard* as the subconscious mind will materialise something that you may not be pleased with.

將不能料敵，以少合眾，以弱擊強，兵無選鋒，曰北。

The General who is not well-versed with the enemy's situation, who employs a small force to fight against a larger one, use a weak force against a strong opponent or who does not select an elite force to occupy the front row is doomed for defeat.

Not knowing that the root of all problems lies within, man usually seeks to correct them without. External effort only forms a small part in defining his final outcome. For example, working hard for money without first correcting the idea of lack in his mind is but a futile attempt, which is *doomed for defeat.*

凡此六者，敗之道也。將之至任，不可不察也。

These are the six ways by which one courts defeat. Therefore, the responsibility lies with the General, who must scrutinise them carefully.

These are the common pitfalls by which *one courts defeat*. You must scrutinise them carefully in order to succeed in your journey towards mastering the mind.

夫地形者，兵之助也。料敵制勝，計險阨遠近，上將之道也。知此而用戰者，必勝；不知此而用戰者必敗。

The nature of the different types of terrains can be of great help to the army. To examine the conditions that can lead the enemy to victory and assess the potential dangers, difficulties and distances are ways of a great General. He who fights in battles with this knowledge is bound to win; he who does not will surely be defeated.

It is the ways of the Master to carefully plan a strategy that will lead him or her to *victory*. A Master of the mind must be well-versed with the nature of the Self and the mind, and the *potential* pitfalls that he or she could face when materialising ideals in his or her experience. The Master will weather through all *difficulties* and *distances* to bring his or her ideals into being. They who can fulfil these are *bound to win* the battle of life and be the Master of their fate, whilst they who do not *will surely be defeated* as they condemn themselves to be victims of their circumstances.

故戰道必勝；主曰：無戰；必戰可也。戰道不勝，主曰必戰，無戰可也。

Therefore, if victory is certain for a battle, even if the Ruler forbids it, the battle must go on; if however one foresees that the battle will end in defeat, one must not fight even if the Ruler commands one to do otherwise.

In this paragraph, Sun Tzu tells you to listen to your inner instincts more than relying on the advice sought from other people. If you know you can succeed, even if the whole world tells you that you cannot, persevere and continue fighting (*the battle must go on*). If however you know that treading on a particular path will not bring you to where you want to be, do not proceed even if others *command* you to do so.

"*When the voice and the vision on the inside become louder than the opinions on the outside, then you have mastered your life.*" (John Demartini)

故進不求名，退不避罪，唯民是保，而利于主，國之寶也。

Therefore, one who acts without seeking for glory or retreats not because of his fear for blame, places the interest of the people before him and serves the sovereign well is indeed a treasure to a nation.

The man who acts out of pure intentions from his heart is indeed a gem, not only to himself but to others as well. He who knows what he truly wants will live a life of purpose and does not concern himself about gaining approval from others. Equanimity is the key to his peace. He treads on the path of righteousness and does what he knows in his heart to be right for he realises that only when he is contented with his life can he be of service to other beings.

視卒如嬰兒，故可與之赴深谿；視卒如愛子，故可與之俱死。厚而不能使，愛而不能令，亂而不能治，譬若驕子，不可用也。

If you look after your soldiers as your children, they will venture with you even to the deepest valleys; regard them like your beloved sons and they will stand by him even in the face of death. However, one who is kind to his men but is unable to exert his authority over them, loving but is unable to enforce one's commands or incapable of managing chaos stemmed from his men is likened to having spoilt children; these men are of no use for the army.

If you nurture the mind just like your own child, it will become the greatest treasure of your life. It will help you weather through difficult times (*venture with you even to the deepest valleys*) and protect you from danger and undesirable situations (*stand by him even in the face of death*). One who does not know how to discipline the mind however will not be able to master his fate and invariably becomes the victim of his circumstances.

"For him who has conquered the mind, the mind is the best of friends; but for one who has failed to do so, his mind will remain the greatest enemy." (Bhagavad Gita)

知吾卒之可以擊，而不知敵之不可擊，勝之半也；知敵之可擊，而不知吾卒之不可擊，勝之半也。知敵之可擊，知吾卒之可以擊，而不知地形之不可以戰，勝之半也。

If you know that your soldiers are ready to strike the enemy but you are unsure whether the conditions on the enemy's side are favourable for you to do so, then the chances of victory is only half.

Similarly, if you are aware that the enemy's condition is favourable for you to attack but you are not convinced that your men are ready to strike, there is also only a half chance of victory. Even if you know that your enemy can be struck and your men are ready to do it, but have not ascertained if the terrain is suitable for battle, this too gives one only a half chance of victory.

According to Sun Tzu, if you are mentally prepared to take on a challenge to secure your goals but do not know the nature the mind, *the chances of victory is only half.* Similarly, if you are merely acquainted with the theory of how the mind works but are not mentally prepared to take any action to work towards your goal, *there is also only a half chance of victory.* Even if you are aware of the powers of the mind and are ready to take action to attain your goals but do not know how to apply the Universal Law in your life, this too gives you *only a half chance of victory.*

It is not enough for one to just know the theory of the Universal Law. Of what use is theoretical knowledge when one does not have practical knowledge? Only by putting what you already know into practice will give you the results you seek.

故知兵者，動而不迷，舉而不窮。故曰：知彼知己，勝乃不殆；知天知地，勝乃可全。

Therefore, one who is well-versed in military matters will not act out of impulse or make a move unprepared. As the saying goes, one who knows the enemy and oneself will not put one's chances of victory at risk. Knowing Heaven and Earth enables one to secure a complete victory.

Conclusively, the Master of the mind will never *act out of impulse*. The Master will remain composed at all times and prepare himself or herself for any challenges that lie ahead in the path that he or she has chosen. Knowing that the mind can be either a friend or foe, the Master will strive to discipline it to achieve only the outcome that he or she desires. They who know that every situation is only a reflection of the ideas they hold in their mind will never be a victim to their circumstances. Understanding the Universal Law and how it can be applied in your daily life will help you *secure a complete victory*.

11 - 九地

NINE GROUNDS

孫子曰：用兵之法，有散地，有輕地，有爭地，有交地，有衢地，有重地，有圮地，有圍地，有死地。諸侯自戰其地者，為散地。入人之地而不深者，為輕地。我得則利，彼得亦利者，為爭地。我可以往，彼可以來者，為交地。諸侯之地三屬，先至而得天下之眾者，為衢地。入人之地深，背城邑多者，為重地。山林、險阻、沮澤，凡難行之道者，為圮地。所由入者隘，所從歸者迂，彼寡可以擊吾之眾者，為圍地。疾戰則存，不疾戰則亡者，為死地。是故散地則無戰，輕地則無止，爭地則無攻，交地則無絕，衢地則合交，重地則掠，圮地則行，圍地則謀，死地則戰。

Sun Tzu said: The Art of War recognises nine different types of grounds:

1) *Crumbling Ground:*
   Where battle is to take place within one's own territory.

2) *Light Ground:*
   Just entering the outskirts of the enemy's territory.

3) *Contentious Ground:*
   Where both parties have equal advantages.

4) *Open Ground:*
   Where any army can freely traverse through.

5) *Intersecting Ground:*
   A junction where there are three adjoining States. The first one to arrive at this junction dominates the support obtained from the masses.

6) *Serious Ground:*
   When one passes through many walled cities to reach the heart of the enemy's territory, one has entered a "serious ground".

7) *Challenging Ground:*
   Mountains, forests, narrow spaces and swamps are paths, which are difficult for the army to pass. These are known as "challenging grounds".

8) *Enclosed Ground:*
   This is one whereby its entrance is narrow and exit is obscure, which allows the enemy to attack one's large group of soldiers by merely using few of his men.

9) *Deadly Ground:*
   On such ground, one survives if one acts without hesitation; otherwise, one dies.

Therefore, one is advised not to battle on a "crumbling ground", not to halt on "light ground", not to attack when on "contentious ground", not to block the enemy's path on "open ground", to join forces with allies on "intersecting ground", to plunder when on "serious ground", to push through "challenging grounds", to rely on strategy when on "enclosed ground" and to fight when on "deadly ground".

In this chapter, Sun Tzu lists the nine different types of mental states that man dwells on in his journey to manifest his ideals in his life experience.

"*Crumbling ground*" is used to describe the state whereby one allows negative ideas to invade one's mind. The seeds (thoughts) that you sow in the divine garden of your mind will become the fruits that you harvest in your life experience. So you must be very selective of the thoughts that you allow to live in your consciousness.

You are entering "*light ground*" when you have taken the first step to re-write circumstances that are unworthy of you. Fearing risks and the possibility of rejection, most people are often afraid of taking the first step towards their goal. Taking the first step is always the hardest one but it will lead you out of your cocoon and bring you towards the life of your dreams. Remember that "*the journey of a thousand miles begins with one single step.*" (Lao Tzu)

"*Contentious ground*" is similar to the "*stalemate ground*" mentioned in the previous chapter. You are treading on such ground when you are unsure of your direction in life. Dwelling on uncertainty allows both positive and negative ideas to have *equal advantages* to occupy your mind.

The mind is on "*open ground*" when it is left idle. Again, as mentioned in the previous chapter, the mind in this state is not subjected to any restrictions as to the nature of thoughts that the mind must dwell on. Sun Tzu says not to "*block the enemy's path*" on this ground. Whenever negative thoughts cross your mind, do not hold on too tightly to them. Just let them pass through. The more you focus on them, the more they linger in your mind and the more power they have over you.

One is stepping into "*intersecting ground*" when the bridge between the conscious mind and the subconscious mind is strong. This state of mind is reached when the body and mind are at rest, making it conducive for you to impress the images you want on the subconscious mind (your best *ally*) to manifest your dreams into reality.

As you move closer towards your goal, you are entering "*serious ground*". This is the critical stage whereby you are almost reaching your destination. Since you have fought for your goal all the way through, do not give up now. Continue maintaining a high mood and persevere until your ideal is objectified.

Life is never void of challenges. It is challenges that shape us to be a stronger person. Overcoming obstacles in your path while manifesting your ideals is to march through "*challenging ground*".

To dwell on limitations is to be entrapped on "*enclosed ground*". Equipped with a negative mental attitude, man fails to open himself to the infinite possibilities that are there in the Universe. If you find yourself dwelling on this state, do your best to set aside all negative thoughts for a moment and devise a *strategy* that can help you achieve your goals. Then, execute the plan accordingly. However, remember not to be too rigid with your initial strategy as unexpected situations may arise.

Any thought that threatens the materialisation of your goal puts you on "*deadly ground*". Your dream will only come true (*survive*) if you believe in its reality. Therefore, be watchful over the ideas that you allow to inhabit your mind. Even when external circumstances threaten your dream, do not fear. Sun Tzu tells you to continue fighting.

古之所謂善用兵者，能使敵人前後不相及，眾寡不相恃，貴賤不相救，上下不相收，卒離而不集，兵合而不齊。

In ancient times, those who were well-versed with the Art of War knew how to divert the attention of the enemy's troops guarding the front and the back, prevent co-operation between the enemy's large and small divisions, hinder the different ranks of officers from helping each other, disrupt the co-ordination between the leaders and their subordinates, cause disorder to compel the enemy's soldiers to leave the army or create division amongst their men and influence the formation of their army so that it is disorganised.

The man who is familiar with the Art of War of the mind will never allow any impurity to taint his mind. He will remove all traces of negativity that exist within him as they may turn against him during his journey in attaining his goals. Instead of being distracted by the negative circumstances that surround him, a true warrior will know how to *divert his attention* back to the goals that he wants to accomplish in life.

合于利而動，不合于利而止。

Act only when there is a desirable advantage. Otherwise, refrain from taking any action.

In this paragraph, Sun Tzu once again emphasises on the importance of evaluating a situation before making a decision to proceed. Know your priorities and think carefully before you act. You are to take action only if it brings you closer to your objectives. Otherwise, *refrain* from indulging yourself in any activity (be it physically or mentally) that brings you nowhere. Time is precious, so invest it wisely.

敢問：「敵眾整而將來，待之若何？」曰：「先奪其所愛，則聽矣；兵之情主速，乘人之不及，由不虞之道，攻其所不戒也。」

Question oneself boldly: "What should I do while waiting for an enemy that has a large army, which is well-formed and headed by a good General, to arrive?"

I say that the answer is: "To first seize something that the enemy holds dear, then he will obey your wishes. Agility is the most important asset in the military. Take the opportunity of catching the enemy off guard by following different routes and attack them in unprotected spots."

As already mentioned several times, the mind can be either one's friend or foe. An undisciplined mind is definitely one's greatest enemy! Since the monkey mind enjoys the privilege of freedom to dwell on any state as it pleases, to curb this freedom by exercising discipline is to "*seize something that (it) holds dear*".

Sun Tzu says that "*agility is the most important asset in the military*". This suggests that one must be *swift* in managing the ever-fluctuating state of the monkey mind. Be ever alert of the thoughts that cross it. When the mind wanders off aimlessly, draw it back (*catch the enemy off guard*) again to focus on the ideal that you desire to experience in your life. There are many *different ways* to discipline the mind and maintain a high mood (a high mood will always draw positive experiences). It can include meditation, chanting, repeating positive affirmations (verbally or by writing), a quiet stroll in the park or even singing. Use whichever way that you find yourself most comfortable with.

凡為客之道，深入則專，主人不克，掠于饒野，三軍足食，謹養而無勞，併氣積力，運兵計謀，為不可測，投之無所往，死且不北，死焉不得，士人盡力。兵士甚陷則不懼，無所往則固，深入則拘，不得已則鬥。

The technique to invade the enemy's land is to enter deep enough into his territory so that he cannot resist your advance. Then, plunder abundant fields along the way so that all three ranks of your army have ample food supply to harness their qi (vital force) so that they have strength. Constantly keep your soldiers on the move and devise your strategies in a way that they cannot be deciphered. Throw your men in situations where there is no escape. Having death or victory as their only options, the soldiers will definitely strive the best they can to evade death. Soldiers trapped in such an extreme situation do not know fear. They will be left with no choice but to stand strong since there is no other way for them to look back. Once the soldiers have entered deep into the enemy's territory, they become more resolute in their mission; when pushed to an extreme, they will fight. Therefore, such men will stay on guard even without prior training and fulfil what is required of them without any prompting. They will also be faithful and trustworthy even without any commands.

If you want to manifest an ideal in your life experience, you will need to go *deep enough* within yourself to build its spiritual structure on the fourth-dimensional plane before it can eventually materialise on this third-dimensional plane.

"*A man is what he thinks about all day long.*" (Ralph Waldo Emerson)

Persistence is the key. You will need to persist in your endeavours until the ideal objectifies. Maintain your enthusiasm to continue on the journey to live the life of your dreams. Feed your soul by doing the things that you love and that which makes you happy to *keep you moving*. Do not stop until the goal is realised.

Sun Tzu again stresses that there is no need for the world to know your intentions (*devise your strategies in a way they cannot be deciphered*). All you have to do is just to continue working towards it and when the time comes, everyone will definitely bear witness to the fruit of the seed that you have planted in your mind. When others are unaware of your goal, there will be less chances for them to discourage you from attaining it. Therefore, be discreet with your plans.

To "*throw your men in situations where there is no escape*" is to centre your mind to dwell one-pointedly on one goal, not allowing it to entertain any other idea. The man who is engrossed only in one ideal knows *no fear*. Staying focused only on one single idea, he sees only one possible path for him to march towards – the goal. This gives him *no other way to look back* and so, he will be *left with no choice but to stand strong* to weather any challenges that may come in his way. That is when your inner strength will really shine. You will never know how strong you are until being strong is the only option you have left.

As you overcome one hurdle after another, your determination to succeed becomes stronger (*become more resolute in their mission*). Even if you lack the knowledge and skills, your strong resolution will somehow bring your will to pass. This is the power one acquires from exercising one-pointedness!

是故，其兵不修而戒，不求而得，不約而親，不令而信，禁祥去疑，至死無所之。

Forbid the interpretation of any omen and remove all doubts; until death, one need not fear any predicted calamity.

Abraham Lincoln says that "*the best way to predict the future is to create it*". Do not give heed to superstitious beliefs. They are only true as long as you give your attention to them. Remember that your destiny is in your hands. Remove all doubts from your mind and focus only on the ideal you desire to objectify. Sun Tzu advises you not to believe in an external power but to believe in yourself. When you have confidence in yourself, you "*need not fear any predicted calamity*" since you allow only yourself to hold the pen to write your life story.

吾士無餘財，非惡貨也；無餘命，非惡壽也。令發之日，士卒坐者涕沾襟，偃臥者涕交頤，投之無所往，則諸劌之勇也。

Just because one's soldiers do not possess excessive wealth does not mean they detest it. Similarly, just because soldiers may not have a long life does not mean they do not wish to live until old age. On the day they are ordered to set out for war, those who are seated will wet their garments with their tears and those lying down will have tears trickling down their cheeks. To cast them into situations where there is no escape will thus provoke them to display the courage of Zhuan Zhu and Cao Kui.

Everyone aspires for something better regardless of whether they expressly admit it or not. To strive for change will however require hard work. You may hesitate to leave your comfort zone, but any change without starts with a change within. Therefore, you will need to detach yourself from your current situation and habits in order to shape your life the way you desire it to be.

Sun Tzu quotes *Zhuan Zhu* and *Cao Kui* whose *courage* and determination are exemplary for all to follow. They were willing to throw themselves into perilous situations in order to fight for their cause. Both clearly knew what they wanted and would allow nothing to come in between them and their goals.

"*We cannot be sure of having something to live for unless we are willing to die for it.*" (Che Guavara)

故善用兵者，譬如率然；率然者，常山之蛇也，擊其首，則尾至，擊其尾，則首至，擊其中，則首尾俱至。敢問：「兵可使如率然乎？」曰：「可。」

Therefore, those skilled in warfare is likened to the "shuai ran" - a serpent found in the Chang mountains. Strike its head, and its tail will attack. Strike its tail, and its head will attack. Strike the middle of its body, and both its head and tail will attack.

If one raises the bold question: "Can the army be transformed to emulate that serpent?"

My answer will be: "Yes!"

In this paragraph, Sun Tzu suggests that man be like the unique *serpent* that is found in the Chang mountains known as the "*shuai ran*". The serpent suggests one not to give in to the temptations that surround you. You must be able to adapt to your varying situations and act accordingly.

The Bible also mentions that "*except you be born again, you cannot enter the kingdom of heaven*". It gives the example that "*as Moses lifted up the serpent in the wilderness, even so must the son of man be lifted up*". In this world of duality, to be 'born' again, you must 'die'. This is Law. The serpent mentioned in the example is no ordinary one. To fully grasp the spiritual significance of the serpent, one must interpret the text fourth-dimensionally. A serpent is a metaphor used to explain the process of endless self-growth. Just like the serpent that sheds its skin without actually physically 'dying', man too should grow spiritually by shedding his old limited beliefs. You 'die' by discarding your current beliefs regarding your circumstances or even life itself so that you may be lifted to the belief of the ideal that you want to be.

夫吳人與越人相惡也，當其同舟濟而遇風，其相救也如左右手。

No matter how much both the colonies of Wu and Yue hated each other, if their men encounter a storm while crossing a river on the same boat, they will still help each other just like how the left hand helps the right hand, and vice versa.

Very often, good and bad experiences give rise to feelings that are miles apart from each other; the good ones promote positive feelings while the bad ones encourage negative feelings. Keep in mind however that your present moment is shaped by your past. Both good and bad experiences are building blocks towards perfection. Every single experience defines your life, so treat both of them alike. Using them as a guide, you should strive to better yourself to exceed the mark that you have set for yourself and learn not to repeat the mistakes of the past.

是故，方馬埋輪，未足恃也，齊勇若一，政之道也；剛柔皆得，地之理也。故善用兵者，攜手若使一人，不得已也。

It is therefore not enough for one to just rely on restraining the horses and burying the wheels. The principle in governing an army is to instil courage equally in all of your men; utilise the surrounding landscape to make the best of both of your strong and weak soldiers. Therefore, one who is well-versed in military affairs will know how to position his soldiers in a way that they are left with no choice but to collaborate with each other as if they are one body.

"*Restraining the horses*" and "*burying the wheels*" intend to prevent soldiers from retreating. Sun Tzu says that the motivation to succeed should not be by force but should instead come from the source of your being. Fighting for a noble purpose that resonates with your heart will *instil courage* within you to endure the journey towards success.

Every little help counts. The man who is skilled in the art of strategy will ensure that he optimises the use of his resources to bring his ideals into being.

將軍之事，靜以幽，正以治，能愚士卒之耳目，使之無知。易其事，革其謀，使人無識，易其居，迂其途，使人不得慮。帥與之期，如登高而去其梯，帥與之深，入諸侯之地而發其機。若驅群羊，驅而往，驅而來，莫知所之。聚三軍之眾，投之于險，此將軍之事也。

It is important that a General remains calm in order to be discreet and be upright to govern the army. He must be able to deceive his soldiers so that they are kept in the dark of the actual plan he has in mind. No one can guess his plans if he constantly alters his method and strategy. Moving campsites and taking unexpected routes also prevent others from deducing his next move. The smart commander leads his troops into a battle in a way that is similar to discarding the ladder of which his men have just climbed up with. He leads them deep into the enemy's territory and only then, signals his intentions. Just like herding a flock of sheep, he directs his men in circles so that they do not know where they are actually heading to. It is the duty of the General to gather all the men from three ranks of the army and cast them into dangerous situations.

Again, Sun Tzu reminds you to be discreet with your movements and strategy. Tell no man about your plan. This includes family and friends. The best evidence that you can present to the world is your success. Otherwise, people will only dismiss your resolution as empty talk. So, just do your best and leave the rest to the Universal Law to objectify your goal.

In ancient battles, a General conceals his plans by remaining calm at all times so as to allow his men to fully focus on their individual duties. A wise General knows that if the men were to fail in their small tasks, the overall strategy will inevitably fail as well. Therefore, this paragraph suggests you to be extremely careful with every step that you take when manifesting your goals for every small step contributes to the larger picture.

Using your mind to shape your circumstances is similar to "*herding a flock of sheep*". Just like how a single sheep that moves causes other sheep to move as well, the act of merely changing one thought in the mind sends out vibrational ripples that will affect the entire Universe, thus resulting in a change of your circumstances. The onus therefore lies with you to direct your thoughts to focus only on the things that you want to see objectified in your experience.

九地之變，屈伸之利，人情之理，不可不察也。

The different types of grounds, advantages of flexibility and adaptability, and the nature of human emotions are important factors that need to be examined.

A warrior of the mind must know all the different states of the mind stated in the above by heart. Along with such knowledge, he must also know how to be flexible in his approaches and learn to adapt to his environment when situation changes. Studying the nature of human emotions will also help him control his mood better so that he attracts to his life only the experiences that he desires. Only by maintaining a high mood can he draw positive experiences.

凡為客之道，深則專，淺則散；去國越境而師者，絕地也；四達者，衢地也；入深者，重地也；入淺者，輕地也；背固前隘者，圍地也；無所往者，死地也。

Bear in mind that the attention of your men, when invading the enemy's ground, become more focused as they move deeper into the territory; otherwise, their attention remains scattered. Leaving one's country behind to cross the border into the enemy's territory with your troops is to enter "dangerous ground". When one arrives at a junction where all four States are connected, this is known as an "intersecting ground". To reach the heart of the enemy's territory is to enter a "serious ground". Remaining on the outskirts of the enemy's territory is to be on "light ground". One is on "enclosed ground" if the soldiers have their backs against solid barriers and have narrow pathways before them. Where there is no way for escape, one is on "deadly ground".

When the senses are focused on physical objects that surround you, your attention is often *scattered*. Only when you begin to journey within yourself that the senses begin to tone down and *become more focused* on one objective. Having tapped into your subconscious mind, you have to be mindful of the impressions that you impregnate it with for you are treading on "*dangerous ground*". Everything that you think of will influence everything in this world to mould itself into the image you hold in your mind.

是故散地吾將一其志，輕地吾將使之屬，爭地吾將趨其後，交地吾將謹其守，衢地吾將固其結，重地吾將繼其食，圮地吾將進其途，圍地吾將塞其闕，死地吾將示之以不活。故兵之情，圍則禦，不得已則鬥，逼則從。

As General, I must therefore lead my men to be one-pointed in their mission when on "crumbling ground", keep the soldiers focused when on "light ground", hurry my troops on "contentious ground", be cautious and remain vigilant while crossing an "open ground", maintain strong bonds with allies when on "intersecting ground", replenish the army's food supply when on "serious ground", push my men to pass through "challenging grounds", block the gaps when on "enclosed ground" and reveal to my soldiers that death awaits them when on "deadly ground".

It is the nature of the army to defend when surrounded, fight when left with no choice and obey commands during critical moments.

Once again, Sun Tzu repeats the list of the different states of the mind and the steps that are to be taken for each.

You, the *General* of your life, must exert your authority when your mind begins to entertain negative ideas on "*crumbling ground*". You are to direct your mind to be "*one-pointed in (your) mission*".

When you have just embarked on the journey to secure your goals, it is very easy to be distracted with other ideas. That is why Sun Tzu says that it is important to be *focused* on your dreams at this stage so that you do not go off-track from your ultimate goal.

You are told to hurry when on "*contentious ground*" because dwelling on uncertainties will lead you nowhere. Delve deep within yourself to find your inner calling and start working towards it.

Be very *cautious* not to leave your mind idle. This state is known in the Art of War as "*open ground*". The mind will wander off to attach itself to any image that it fancies, which also includes negative thoughts. Therefore, remain *vigilant* and keep watch of your mental activity at all times. As soon as you find yourself entertaining any negativity, slowly draw it back to your goal.

Remember that your physical reality is a reflection of your mental world. To change anything on the outside requires a change from within. Therefore, *maintain a strong bond* with your best ally – the subconscious mind. Once you can convince your subconscious mind that an idea is real, the idea will definitely objectify in your experience.

You are treading on "*serious ground*" as you advance nearer to your goal. While you must continue to focus on completing the journey, do also the things that will feed your soul to renew your zeal for life. The feeling of happiness always draws pleasant experiences, which may motivate you further to accomplish your goal and even set bigger ones.

Do not give up when you face obstacles in life (*challenging ground*). Push through the challenges that come your way. Celebrating minor victories helps remind yourself of your capabilities. People often aim high but they do not realise that it will take some time for the ideal to come to pass. Just like a seed that needs time and nurturing to grow into a tree, an idea also requires time and effort before it can objectify itself in your world. It is due to impatience that people usually give up on their dreams. This is how most people usually give in to the challenges they come across in life.

Sun Tzu reminds you that you should never entertain limiting ideas. That is why he says to *block the gaps* when on "*enclosed ground*". Do not allow a single trace of negativity to linger in your mind or it shall harden into fact as your circumstances.

Should any thought threaten the manifestation of your ideal, you are on "*deadly ground*". If you find yourself getting demotivated by negative thoughts and feel tempted to give up on your dream, present yourself with two choices: to succeed or to fail. Reminding yourself of the disappointment and consequences that come with the unfulfilled dream will give newfound strength to continue fighting.

是故不知諸侯之謀者，不能預交，不知山林險阻沮澤之形者，不能行軍，不用鄉導者，不能得地利，此三者不知一，非霸王之兵也。

Therefore, those who do not know the strategy of other feudal lords cannot secure their alliances. Those who are not familiar with the terrains of the mountains, forests, defiles, gorges and wetlands cannot lead their troops through them. Not employing native guides, one cannot benefit from the natural advantages that the grounds can offer. One who does not know these three rules by heart is not fit to be known as a warlord.

Wisdom is necessary if one were to succeed in life. Just as highlighted in Chapter 7, it never hurts to seek advice from other experienced people. Their words may give you a clearer insight as to how you can adopt a positive mental attitude in order to materialise your ideals. They can share with you the mental strategy that they have devised and applied successfully into their lives. This is how you "*secure the alliances (from other) feudal lords*".

夫霸王之兵，伐大國則其眾不得聚，威加于敵，則其交不得合。是故不爭天下之交，不養天下之權，信己之私，威加于敵，故其城可拔，其國可墮。

When a warlord attacks a powerful kingdom, he will be able to prevent the enemy from congregating to join forces. A warlord's power overwhelms the enemy so much so that even the enemy's allies cannot come to their rescue. Therefore, there is no need for him to strive to form allies with other nations, nor does he need to foster their influence. The warlord has complete confidence in his own strategy that it intimidates the enemy. With that, he is able to conquer their cities and cause the downfall of their empire.

This paragraph is all about being independent. Develop a strong character so that nothing can stop you from fulfilling your dreams. Where there is a will, there is always a way. If you have faith in your vision (*confidence in his own strategy*), there will be no need to plead others to help you in your mission for they will naturally feel compelled from within to do so. Everything will fall into place at the perfect time.

施無法之賞，懸無政之令，犯三軍之眾，若使一人。犯之以事，勿告以言；犯之以利，勿告以害；投之亡地然後存，陷之死地然後生。

Bestow rewards beyond the scope of established rules and give out commands beyond the scope of established policies; treat all the three ranks of your army as you would treat an individual person, instruct and teach your men with actions and incidents but not with words, and motivate them with the advantages that can be acquired but tell them nothing of any possible harm. Cast your army into dangerous situations and your men will survive. Plunge them into "deadly ground" and they will survive.

Sun Tzu has always shown an aversion for a rigid framework of rules and practices. While it is important for society to be governed by rules to distinguish a right from a wrong, it should serve only as a general guideline. No established rules should define your life. Do not let them hinder you from dreaming the extraordinary life that you were born to live. You are the dreamer who dreams your life into being. Therefore, dream the best life you can ever imagine even if it is deemed impossible by others.

Actions speak louder than words. Instruct your mind by tapping into your subconscious mind to imagine vividly the wish as having been fulfilled is more effective than merely uttering positive words. Put the Universal Law to the test and experience the power of the mind yourself. One single experience outweighs all the bookish knowledge that you have gained over the years as theory is now transformed into practice.

Be the bearer of good news. See and hear only the good in everything. Reject from your consciousness anything that you deem unlovely. Learn from the example of Jesus Christ who only acknowledged the goodness in all given situations.

Walking past a dead dog on the street that was already emanating a foul smell, everyone cried that it should be taken away and be burnt. Instead of joining the commotion, Jesus just smiled and praised the beauty of the dog's white teeth. Similarly, you are to focus only on the positive aspects and reject from your consciousness all negative suggestions. This is how you will triumph over negative circumstances and be victorious in your endeavours to realise your goals.

夫眾陷于害，然後能為勝敗，故為兵之事，在于順詳敵之意，併力一向，千里殺將，是謂巧能成事。

Troops that have fallen into harm's way can turn defeat into victory. What is of utmost importance to the army lies in discerning the enemy's intentions and ensuring that troops remain one-pointed in their mission to kill the enemy's General who is one thousand li away. This is how an ingenious accomplishes his goal.

The first step towards success is to admit your mistakes. Only by learning from your past can you *"turn defeat into victory"*.

"A man must be big enough to admit his mistakes, smart enough to profit from them, and strong enough to correct them." (John C. Maxwell)

If you have never committed any mistake, you have never tried anything new. Mistakes are inevitable. The smartest people are not the ones who do not make mistakes but the ones who make mistakes and learn from them to steer themselves towards perfection.

Never let your mistakes hinder your progress. While you should learn from them, focus one-pointedly on your mission to *accomplish your goals*. Forget failures. Forget mistakes. Forget everything except the very thing that you are supposed to do now and just do it!

是故政舉之日，夷關折符，無通其使，厲于廊廟之上，以誅其事，敵人開闔，必亟入之。先其所愛，微與之期，賤墨隨敵，以決戰爭。是故始如處女，敵人開戶，後如脫兔，敵不及拒。

Therefore, on the day you receive the official statement, block the borders, destroy official tallies and do not allow their emissaries to pass through. Assume control over the situation by being strict in the imperial court and execute your plans accordingly. Should the enemy leave a door open, rush in. First seize what the enemy holds dear and keep the time of battle hidden. Adapt to the enemy's situation and make use of it to plan your move in battles. And so, begin a battle by exhibiting coyness and innocence like a maiden until the enemy lets his guard down. Then, like a running hare, quickly seize the opportunity to attack the enemy. By then, he will not be able to resist your advance.

Therefore, the moment you resolute to achieve something, cast away all doubts, anxiety and fear. Assume your role as the Mastermind of the situation and be watchful over the thoughts that you allow to cross your mind. *Execute your plans* by doing only the things that will make your goals become a reality. To be "*strict in the imperial court*" symbolises working with the Self. There is no "*court*" more royal than the realm of the Self. Decide your goals carefully and work towards them. As soon as you notice an opportunity that will bring you to your goal, take it! Nonetheless, remember to never compromise your goal with something lesser than what you really want.

First seize the freedom of your mind to wander aimlessly as it pleases and be discreet of your intentions. Tell no man of your goals. Adapt yourself to your current circumstances while waiting for your ideals to objectify. Observe the situation and act accordingly. Carefully *plan your move* throughout the battle.

Sun Tzu suggests you begin your journey by "*exhibiting coyness and innocence like a maiden until the enemy lets his guard down*". Staying silent about your motives helps get you through the battle more easily since you need not face unnecessary resistance from naysayers that may distract you from fulfilling your dreams. Since the entire world operates mentally, your ideas will subtly influence those around you to bring your vision into reality as "*(they) will not be able to resist your advance*". When the opportunity presents itself, be "*like a running hare… to quickly seize (it)*" and change your life to be what you want it to be!

12 - 火攻

ATTACK WITH FIRE

孫子曰：凡火攻有五：一曰火人，二曰火積，三曰火輜，四曰火庫，五曰火隊。

Sun Tzu said: There are five ways by which one can use fire to attack:

1) *To burn a person,*
2) *To burn provisions,*
3) *To burn military wagons,*
4) *To burn warehouses, and*
5) *To burn an entire unit of army.*

In spirituality, the symbol of fire signifies effulgence and illumination. It is used to show the transformation of man from darkness (ignorance) to light (Truth).

Fire has been used in religious rites since time immemorial. It is also one of the five sacred elements in Hinduism. Followers of the Hindu faith believe that the entire creation is made of these five elements. Hindus also consider fire as an essential eternal witness to sacred religious ceremonies.

The Zoroastrian religion also uses fire to represent the Ahura Mazda (God of the Zoroastrians). For them, fire is considered as the sacred and supreme symbol of God; a divine symbol in any act of sacrifice.

Where there is fire, there is light. The Bible states that "God is light" and the Upanishads declare that "Brahman is Jyotirmaya" (Brahman is full of light). Therefore, fire has a very important place in one's spiritual journey.

"Except you be born again, you cannot enter the kingdom of heaven." (John 3:3)

When man's limited ego is consumed by the spiritual fire, he is reborn. This is what the term "sacrifice" really means. Only with wisdom can man attain a spiritual rebirth so that he knows the Self and understands the nature of the mind.

However, before you can be 'born' again, you must first 'die'; this is Law. You 'die' by discarding your current beliefs regarding your current circumstances or even life itself so that you may be lifted to the belief of the ideal you want to be.

When you have acquired spiritual wisdom of the Self, you realise your true nature: *"He appeared to put away sin by the sacrifice of himself."* (Hebrews 9:26)

Man's limited ego-self is nothing but the sum total of all that he believes and consents to as true.

"I will become what I know I am." (Michael Jordan)

According to Sun Tzu's principles of fire attacks, the stages that man goes through when sacrificing his old concepts of the ego-self to replace them with new ideals so that they dominate his consciousness are as follow:

1) *"To burn a person":*

If your current reality is not what you would like to experience in life, you will then need to replace the concept of your existence in this Universe. Do not keep the ideas in your mind that sustain this reality. Seek for ideals that are worthy of you, which resonate with your heart and sacrifice all the beliefs that suggest otherwise. If you want something else, you must be willing to give up what you are now in order to be what you want to be.

2) *"To burn provisions":*

Eliminate from your consciousness all that feed the old concepts of the self that you no longer want to be acquainted with. Do not sustain old ideas that you do not desire to experience on this physical plane. Eradicate all negative thoughts and feelings from your consciousness. Cut off all possible roots that may feed your negative approaches to life.

For example, if your current reality is sustained by feeding on your fear, then vanquish fear from your consciousness once and for all. After all, F.E.A.R. is nothing but 'False Evidences Appearing Real'. There is nothing to fear but fear itself! Conduct a mental assessment and decide which qualities should be kept and which should be discarded.

Check your surroundings to see if anything in your environment suggests that your dream has not been fulfilled. Feng Shui expert Marie Diamond reminds you to *"remember (that) you are the Creator of your Universe, and your home and office is part of your Universe."*

Your physical surroundings are the reflection of your inner deepest thoughts. Regardless of whatever desire that you hold within yourself, see and feel that it has materialised in your objective experience. Arrange your physical environment in preparation for the ideal to materialise on this objective plane.

3) *"To burn military wagons":*

We cannot expect everyone to see the world the same way we do. Our ways and beliefs may not always be accepted by others the way we hope them to be. Nonetheless, the rejection from other people should never be an excuse for one not to live up to their ideals. Regardless of whether or not others respect your beliefs and objectives, respect theirs for everyone has their own path but do not allow their negative suggestions to affect your journey in attaining your goals.

No matter how strongly others oppose the mission you have set for yourself, if you feel that you are worthy of it, then persevere and continue on your path towards its realisation. Do not be moved by their words and actions. Release all criticisms and cynicisms from your mind. This is how you *burn* the enemy's *military wagons* that they use to destroy your dreams.

4) "To burn warehouses":

Find the very root of the limited beliefs that you hold within. At this stage, dare to challenge your limits. If fear is what is holding you back, dare yourself to surpass that feeling.

For example, if you are afraid of heights, do not let your fear stop you from achieving your goals regardless of how small or big they may be. Perhaps your dream is to one day be a successful pilot. Due to your fear of heights however, you hesitate to take the initiative to sign up for flying lessons. Be assured that there is nothing in this world to be afraid of except fear itself! You are confronting your fears when you do the very things you are afraid of. Having faced the devil, its power over you diminishes and over time, the fear of flying will cease from your consciousness.

With each fear you conquer, your mental aptitude increases. Fear will eventually have no place in your consciousness as you grow out of it; you would have burned this *warehouse* (source) of fear.

This practice does not apply only to one's efforts in conquering fear. Any trace of other negative qualities within you does not draw positive results. The Bible advises to *"do unto others as you would have others do unto you."* Annihilate the root of negativity in your mind. This includes that of selfishness, greed, anger, jealousy, hatred and other negative traits. Remember, what you give is what you will get. man is simply incapable of receiving love if hatred dominates his consciousness. Similarly, he is incapable of receiving monetary wealth if the idea of lack, which compels him to act selfishly, is strongly enrooted in his mind. Therefore, send out good thoughts and practice good actions, and you are sure to receive equivalent results.

5) "To burn an entire unit of army":

The moment you realise your goal, you will silent all the naysayers who once believed that your dream was an impossible mission. If no other individual has ever lived your dream before, you will then establish a new precedent that it is possible. Observing your successful mission, others will begin to accept its possibility and alter their concepts and feelings in relation to that goal. Hence, _"an entire unit_ of (the opposition's) _army"_ would have been burned as they discover that the concepts they once believed in are no longer relevant for this new paradigm established by you.

行火必有因，煙火必素具。發火有時，起火有日。時者，天之燥也。日者，月在箕壁翼軫也。凡此四宿者，風起之日也。

To attack with fire requires proper conditions and basic equipments. There are suitable time and day to set fire. The most suitable time is when the weather is dry. The most suitable day is when the moon aligns with the constellations of Ji (Sagittarius), Bi (Andromeda), Yi (Crater) and Zhen (Corvus). These are the four days when the wind rises.

One must be equipped with the _basic_ wisdom of the Self and the nature of the mind in order to use the Universal Law to one's advantage. Spiritual wisdom is crucial in the art of mastering of the mind.

Sun Tzu's definition of _"suitable time"_ is to employ Mother Nature's way to work to one's advantage.

In any physical battle, fire is ideally used as a weapon to attack the enemy _when the weather is dry_. A dry condition allows objects to easily catch fire. Therefore, one can use the knowledge of the way how Mother Nature works to one's benefit. Similarly, the most conducive state for man to invoke his creative faculty to rearrange his worldly experiences is to tap into his natural state of being. This state is the core of his existence. Man experiences this state when the chatter of his mind is silenced either through meditation or when he is about to fall asleep.

"In a dream, in a vision of the night, when deep sleep falleth upon men, in slumbering upon the bed; then he openeth the ears of men and sealeth their instructions." (Job 33:14-16)

The way to pray effectively is to silence the mind from chatters and creatively visualise the end result that you would like objectified on the physical plane. This state is best because the bridge between your conscious and subconscious is at its strongest. It allows man to enter the subconscious to make his impressions to alter the conditions and events of his life.

Sun Tzu also mentions about the *"most suitable day when the moon aligns with the constellations of Ji, Bi, Yi and Zhen"*. The moon is often used as a symbol of the mind. Hindu deity Lord Shiva is depicted as wearing the crescent moon on His head, suggesting that He is in complete control of the mind. Instead of being enslaved by the mind, He has mastered it.

"When the moon aligns with the (four) constellations" are the *four days when the wind rises.* Interpreted fourth-dimensionally, man must learn to achieve a balance between the conflicts that exist within him. This is clearly portrayed through the constellation of *Sagittarius*, who is identified in Greek mythology as a centaur. This powerful imagery of half-man and half-horse symbolises the conflict between the mind and body, intellect and instinct, and the animal and spiritual qualities. Only the man who knows how to maintain the

balance between these conflicting aspects will be able to master his mind.

He must also recognise the quality of *Andromeda*, known as the Goddess of fertility, which is within him.

"*The Lord said to the woman, I will greatly multiply your sorrow and in pain you shall bring forth children, yet your desire shall be for your husband and he shall rule over you.*" (Genesis 3:16)

This biblical verse should not be read literally. The word "*children*" does not refer to the babies that come from the womb of a woman, but states brought forth from your mind. Any state that you dwell on in your mind, be it positive or negative, will objectify as your life experience. They become your children.

Crater is the Latin term for goblet belonging to the Greek God Apollo. Spiritually, a goblet signifies the 'Cup of Life'. The mind is an instrument that reflects man's divinity. It is with this 'Cup of Life' (the mind) that you can fill it up with whatever you desire, but be reminded that the very thing you fill it up with is what your life will be.

The *Corvus* is a small constellation, which Latin name stands for raven. Ravens symbolise spiritual strength and have a long history of myth and lore associated with them. Some believe ravens to be the 'keeper of universal secrets'. There are native tribes who even worship ravens as the creator of the world. Therefore, when man realises that he is none other than the creator of his own reality, he will not allow anyone or anything else to determine what he can or cannot achieve in life.

The "*wind*" is the symbol of swiftness in movement. When you have the qualities of all the *four constellations* as stated in the above, there are no obstacles that can impede you from living your ideals on this objective plane. Just like how the *wind* helps spread the fire when you attack the enemy's camp, these qualities will allow you to endure all challenges and increase the magnitude of your spiritual influence in re-arranging the Universe to fulfil all your desires.

凡火攻，必因五火之變而應之，火發于內，則早應之于外。火發而其兵靜者，待而勿攻。極其火力，可從而從之，不可從而止。火可發于外，無待于內，以時發之。火發上風，無攻下風，晝風久，夜風止。

Generally in fire attacks, one must respond accordingly to five possible developments.

1) *If fire is started in the enemy's camp, quickly attack them from the outside.*
2) *If the enemy's camp is on fire but they are not aware of it or choose to remain still, then wait and do not attack them first.*
3) *Allow the fire to reach its height and attack the enemy where you can but do not proceed where you cannot.*
4) *If conditions and time are favourable for one to set fire from the outside, there is no need to wait to start one inside.*
5) *Attack using fire when the wind rises but refrain from using it when there is no wind. The day breeze usually lasts longer than the night breeze.*

When you live your ideals, you become the living example for the principles of the Self. You will invoke other people's curiosity in the Universal Law, which can be applied in their lives so that they too can experience the ideals they desire.

This is the work of the Spirit to help make this world a better place for everyone to live in.

"Don't grow only for yourself. If you have some worthwhile information, share it. By reaching others, you will reach yourself." (Rabbi Noah Weinberg)

The following are the *five principles* that will guide you in your role as the warrior of Light:

1) Since living a life of your ideals will ignite the fire of curiosity within the ignorant man, he will begin enquiring within himself why you are able to achieve your goals while he cannot.

   According to Mental Science, Sun Tzu's phrase to *"attack (the enemy) from the outside"* when *"...fire is started in the enemy's camp"* does not signify physical violence. The ignorant man struggles with conflicting ideas of lack and abundance. Witnessing your example, he will try to reason and preserve the old limiting belief system that he has been brought up with. As he struggles within with the newly acquired wisdom (or *fire*) of the Self, let your success on the physical plane be a proof to him of the infallible Universal Law.

2) If the *fire* of spiritual wisdom is already ignited within the heart of the ignorant man, there is no need to do anything else but to allow the fire to slowly consume his being to release him from the bondage of this illusory world. Regardless of whether or not he is *aware* of this spiritual transformation, the sleeping man will eventually come to realise that within him, lies the only true power - the Self.

3) Strive for the *fire* of spiritual wisdom to burn brightly within you. Allow this *fire* to engulf your entire being and let it direct your thoughts, words and deeds. Equipped with this eternal wisdom of the Self, you can be sure that you will never go astray. You will allow nothing to shake your faith in the reality of your vision.

Reflecting the Truth of the Self with your own life, you will also help ignite this fire of wisdom within others. Help eradicate limiting beliefs in the mind of the sleeping man. Assist those who are earnest to learn the Truth of the Self so that they too are liberated from misery caused by attachment to the illusion of matter. However, do not impose your ideas on those who are not ready *(do not proceed where you cannot)*. As mentioned earlier, respect other people's choices even if they do not view life the same way that you do.

"Whoever does not receive you, nor heed your words, as you go out of that house or that city, shake the dust off your feet." (Luke 9:3-5)

Be a light to those who are ready to open themselves to receive the wisdom of the Universal Law, but do not be moved by those who ridicule your ideas.

4) To awaken a sleeping man can be an arduous task. Whether it is others or oneself, knowledge of the Self remains merely a theory that is yet to be experienced. Only by experience can one fully appreciate the Truth of it. So, put the principles to practice and test the Universal Law yourself. Your faith will be increased when you experiment; when you test this Law.

"Examine yourselves to see whether you are in the faith; test yourselves. Do you not realise that Christ Jesus is in you - unless, of course, you fail the test?" (2 Corinthians 13:5)

Act and evidence will always follow. Persuade yourself to see your vision as true and it will come true. When you show others how you live your life based on these principles, you are *setting the fire* of wisdom from the outside so that in time, their curiosity to test the Universal Law will lead the fire to burn from within.

5) For the *wind* to rise, the conditions listed above must be fulfilled. You can inspire others with the eternal wisdom of the Self only when you have fulfilled the criteria symbolically represented by the constellations of *Ji (Sagittarius), Bi (Andromeda), Yi (Crater) and Zhen (Corvus)* as mentioned earlier in this chapter. Speaking of the Universal Law to others remains a lip service when one does not live by it.

"Day" signifies the Light or awakening, while *"night"* symbolises ignorance. The Truth is permanent while ignorance is just a temporary phase of the absence of light. All it requires is one ray of Light to expel darkness. That is what Sun Tzu means by the *"day breeze usually lasts longer than the night breeze"*.

凡軍必知五火之變，以數守之。故以火佐攻者明，以水佐攻者強，水可以絕，不可以奪。

All armies need to thoroughly understand the five possible developments of using fire attacks and use calculations to apply the technique effectively. Therefore, those who use fire to aid their attack are indeed intelligent. On the other hand, those who use the water factor to attack will only give them strength over the enemy because water supply, though can be cut, cannot be used to conquer.

Warriors of Light must *understand* these five strategies to help awaken the eternal *fire* of wisdom of the Universal Law in the hearts of men. Those who know how to rely on this *fire* of spiritual wisdom, the Universal Law, are not only *intelligent*, but also wise.

Sun Tzu's phrase of "*cutting (the enemy's) water supply*" revolves around the idea of lack; to deprive another of something. This conjures the image of suppressing others for one's own benefit. When man acts thus, he is holding onto a concept within his mind that there are limited resources available for everyone to utilise. Operating from such a limited belief will only bestow him *strength* over others temporarily, but denies him from experiencing greater abundance in life.

Sun Tzu is of the opinion that man does not gain true victory in this way since the law of deprivation *cannot be used to conquer* his being to make him the Master of his own fate for his mind is imbued with the ideas of deficiency.

夫戰勝攻取，而不修其攻者凶，命曰費留。故曰：明主慮之，良將修之，非利不動，非得不用，非危不戰。

They who attack, conquer and gain victory in a battle but do not develop their skills are wasting their lives as they remain stagnant. Therefore, it is said that while an intelligent General will contemplate on this, a virtuous one will put these principles into practice; do not act unless there is an advantage to secure, do not employ the troops unless there is something to gain from it and do not battle unless there is a critical need for it.

Sun Tzu advises that learning is a never-ending journey. He encourages all to continuously develop one's skill and expand one's knowledge. There is always room for improvement. To *remain stagnant* is to *waste one's life*. While those acquainted with the wisdom of the Self are *intelligent*, only the wise and *virtuous* man will put the wisdom he has learnt into practice.

Remain steadfast to your vision. Do not compromise with anything lesser than your goal.

For example, let's say what you want is a particular model of car, do not settle for any other just because your circumstances tell you that you cannot possibly obtain it. Envision in your mind's eye that you are now driving that car. Engage all your five inner senses to experience the car as yours and circumstances without will begin to change to bring your vision into reality. Even if a good offer comes your way for another model, do not settle for it. Have faith in your vision for an assumption though false, if persisted in will harden into fact.

Therefore, *do not act* unless your actions bring your dream into fruition.

主不可以怒而興師，將不可以慍而致戰；合于利而動，不合于利而止。怒可以復喜，慍可以復悅，亡國不可以復存，死者不可以復生。故明君慎之，良將警之，此安國全軍之道也。

A Ruler should never dispatch his troops solely because of anger and a General should also not declare war just because of resentment. Act only if there is an advantage that is relevant to one's interest. If there is not any, then stop. It is just a matter of time when the angry can become happy again and the hurt can be pleased, but a destroyed nation can never be restored to exist again and the dead can never come back to life. Therefore, a wise Ruler will act with care and a respectable General will remain cautious at all times. This is the Path to protect a nation and keep the army intact.

Anger is the greatest enemy that can lead to self-destruction. This quality is likened to an intoxicant that compels man to make brash and unwise decisions.

"Holding on to anger is like grasping a hot coal with the intent of throwing it at someone else; you are the one who gets burned." (Gautama Buddha)

Anger is a weakness of the mind. To harness spiritual strength, one must therefore remove anger by instilling positive thoughts and feelings.

When you are faced with a situation that angers you, distract your mind to focus on 'seeing' only the good side of it. This is how you see no evil, hear no evil and speak no evil.

Do not waste your energy getting angry over things that bring you nowhere. Acting out of impulse is a mere waste of inner resources. Ensure that all your actions are *relevant* to objectifying your goals into reality. Time is precious. Discard all habits and practices that do not bring you nearer to the attainment of your objectives. If to be a published author is your dream, then indulging in idle gossips or watching television is a waste of time. The time spent on these futile actions can instead be better invested in finding resources or gaining inspiration by reading the works of other authors to produce the book.

Do not respond to criticisms or negative situations just because you feel threatened. All feelings are momentary and they too, shall come to pass. A wrong move compelled by emotions can lead to a disastrous outcome, which damage can possibly never be undone.

Therefore, a wise man will always remain vigilant of his thoughts, words and deeds. He will contemplate on the consequences of his every action before making a move. This is the key to experiencing peace within, which is essential for one to maintain the right mindset to achieve one's goals. To remain composed allows one to harness spiritual strength that can be directed towards worthy objectives. Martin Luther King Jr. believes that "*peace is not merely a distant goal that we seek but a means by which we arrive at that goal.*"

13 - 用間
USING SPIES

孫子曰：凡興師十萬，出征千里，百姓之費，公家之奉，日費千
金，內外騷動，怠于道路，不得操事者，七十萬家，相守數年，
以爭一日之勝，而愛爵祿百金，不知敵之情者，不仁之至也，非
人之將也，非主之佐也，非勝之主也。故明君賢將，所以動而勝
人，成功出于眾者，先知也；先知者，不可取于鬼神，不可象于
事，不可驗于度；必取于人，知敵之情者也。

*Sun Tzu said: Generally, to dispatch a hundred thousand men to go
into battle a thousand li away will entail heavy expenses on the
citizen and drain the State's resources. Not only the daily
expenditure will be one thousand pieces of gold, there will be
commotion inside out, people neglected by the roadsides and people*

are unable to do their daily chores. Seven hundred families will be struggling together with the army for many years until victory is gained one day.

Those who are obsessed with ranks and wealth but remain ignorant of the enemy's situation are inhumane; such a person cannot be a leader of men, an assistant to the Ruler or the Master of victory. Therefore, a wise Ruler and a good General can achieve success beyond ordinary men as he secures victory with every move using foreknowledge; foreknowledge cannot be elicited from ghosts or the Gods, developed from experience or verified by any system. Foreknowledge can only be obtained from people who are aware of the enemy's situation.

Conflicts drain energy and incur losses in various ways. Man continues to struggle amidst conflicts until the day a solution is found. We are all connected as there is only one force pervading the entire Universe. Conflicts therefore do not only affect the individual alone, but also other people.

Sun Tzu classifies the people *who are obsessed with ranks and wealth* (which insinuates the ego) as *"inhumane"*. In other words, those who react and fight merely to preserve their reputation is simply unfit to *be a leader of men, an assistant to the Ruler or the master of victory*. It is due to ego that individuals attempt to exercise their authority over others, thinking that their perception alone is true. He suggests that one can secure *success beyond other ordinary men* only by the use of *foreknowledge* (foresight), which cannot be gained from an external source or superstitious beliefs. The ability to foresee something can only be gained through awareness and experience, and this is possible through the employment of the mental *spy*.

As already mentioned in the earlier chapters of this book, do not be despaired if your surrounding reality denies you of the ideal that you desire to experience. All you have to do is to employ the services Rahab (translated as the Spirit), a spy and harlot, to secure the state of your ideal, which the Bible calls it Jericho. A harlot is one who grants you anything you ask for and a spy has the ability to travel discreetly to locations without being discovered.

Whatever ideal you desire, employ the services of Rahab to manifest it in your experience. The Bible says to "*pray in secret*". So, shut your five external senses and turn within. Direct your thoughts to dwell on the state that you wish to materialise in your physical reality. You can assume to be anywhere and be anyone you want to be in your mind. No one will ever know where you are mentally dwelling. If you feel fulfilled after your attention returns to your physical surroundings, it means that this assumption has been registered in your subconscious mind, which when persisted in, will objectify into actual fact. This is what we know as "faith". Faith is not something that can be developed from observing your physical *experiences* nor can it *be verified by any system*. The faith in your vision is what gives you the *foreknowledge* that the day will arrive when you will physically experience the ideal you so desire.

Equipped with faith, you are sure to create miracles in your life and *achieve success beyond ordinary men*.

故用間有五：有鄉間、有內間、有反間、有死間、有生間。五間俱起，莫知其道，是謂神紀，人君之寶也。鄉間者，因其鄉人而用之。內間者，因其官人而用之。反間者，因其敵間而用之。死間者，為誑事于外，令吾間知之，而傳于敵。生間者，反報也。

There are five different types of spies that may be employed:
1) *A native*
2) *An undercover*
3) *A traitor*
4) *A dead spy*
5) *A surviving spy*

When these five types of spies are used together, there is none who can discover their objectives. This is what we call by a "secret service", a treasure to a kingdom.

To employ a native spy, one must use a local villager who is from that area. An undercover spy must be a high-ranking official working for the enemy's government. A traitor is turning the enemy's spy into one's own. Employing 'dead spies' means to create a scene to transmit deceiving messages to our own spies so that they can pass it to the enemy. 'Surviving spies' are those who physically return to base with news from the enemy's camp.

Begin constructing the structure of your ideal on the fourth-dimensional plane by feeling that your ideal has already been fulfilled. Below are the five mental *spies* that can help you get into the spirit of living the ideal in your mind. Employ these five *mental spies* and be assured that your potential to achieve any goal is limitless. This is the "*secret service*" that is a treasure to your kingdom for the "*kingdom of heaven is within you*" (Luke 17:21).

1) Native:

Obtain as much information as possible about the ideal that you would like to materialise in your experience. Follow in the footsteps of the people who are already there, living the goals that you wish to achieve.

"Birds of the same feather flock together." (English idiom)

It is best to surround yourself with people who remind you of your ideals. One can tell a lot about a person by seeing the company they keep. If you would like to lead a positive and happy life, do not surround yourself with negative and unhappy people.

2) Undercover:

If you find it difficult to feel as though you are already living your ideal, then do all that is necessary to encourage the feelings of its reality. If buying a house is what you want, go out and actually find your dream home and walk through it several times to get into the feeling of already owning it. The same principle applies to any other objects that you wish to materialise in life. Remember, all that you desire are not things that are separate from you. They are mere ideas, which when focused on will objectify in your experience.

3) Traitor:

The people who once lived with the common concept that they have no role to play in shaping their circumstances, but who now know that they do, can be known as *"traitors"* since they are no longer confined within societal norms or expectations. These are the best people whom you can seek advice from since they will understand the struggles that you may be going through with the concepts of Mental Science. They are most likely to have been in your position before and are therefore able to offer invaluable insights pertaining to the Universal Law and guide you to overcome any mental blockage that you may be experiencing in objectifying your ideals.

4) Dead Spy:

Employing a "d*ead spy*" is to ensure that your environment reflects the idea that your desire has already materialised in your experience. This is how you *create a scene to transmit deceiving messages* through your five physical senses to your conscious mind so that the idea of its fulfilment can be impregnated on your subconscious mind. Once the idea fills your subconscious mind, you are sure to experience it in the flesh.

5) Surviving Spy:

Rahab (the Spirit) is the "*surviving spy*". When you close your eyes to visualise your ideal, you are breaking the walls of physical reality that defies you of its fulfilment.

According to the Bible, Rahab was specifically instructed not to hop from house to house but to make her way to the upper room of the house, which she has entered at the heart of the city. She was to remain there as the walls of Jericho crumbled.

Nature abhors a vacuum. When an ideal is alive in your consciousness, your physical reality cannot be void of it. Therefore, the state that you send Rahab to dwell in within your mind will destroy any walls that separate you from your ideal.

故三軍之事，親莫親于間，賞莫厚于間，事莫密于間，非聖智不能用間，非仁義不能使間，非微妙不能得間之實。微哉，微哉，無所不用間也。間事未發而先聞者，間與所告者皆死。

And so, in all the three ranks of the armies combined, there is no one who is treasured more than a spy, rewarded more generously than a spy and must act more discreetly than a spy. Those who lack the sacred wisdom cannot use spies, those not benevolent and righteous are unable to employ spies and those who are not subtle cannot obtain the Truth from spies. Profound indeed is the art of employing spies as there is nothing for which one cannot use them. If the spy's identity and activities are divulged before the mission is accomplished, then the spy and those who have been told of the matter should be put to death.

The practice of relying on the services of *Rahab* is by far the most important aspect in the art of mastering one's mind. When you have mastered your mind, you become the Master of your circumstances.

Sun Tzu however suggests that there are various criteria to satisfy before one can actually *use spies*:

The first criterion that he highlighted is the need for "*sacred wisdom*". Those *who lack the sacred wisdom* simply do not know the merits of using Rahab to help them manifest their goals in their physical experience.

Secondly, those who would like to *employ spies* must be *benevolent* and *righteous*. Non-violence is the prime characteristic of a *benevolent* soul. Any form of external opposition that has the potential to harm another, be it physically or mentally, is practicing violence. As Spirit operates on the basis of love and oneness, to inflict harm on another is to inflict harm on oneself. Any evil that you imagine for other people harms you than it does them for

Mahatma Gandhi says, "*man is but the product of his own thoughts; what he thinks, he becomes.*"

People who use their thoughts with an intention to inflict harm on another dwell on ideas of lack. Therefore, employing Rahab for such destructive purposes will not confer them the happiness they seek.

Righteousness is the consciousness of already being what you desire to be; that is to say you experience the ideal as having already objectified in your physical reality the way you want it to. Those who are not *righteous* do not employ Rahab to dwell in the state that they would like to experience in their physical reality.

Throughout the entire Art of War literature, Sun Tzu emphasises on being "*subtle*" in one's approaches when working towards a goal. Its importance is clearly observed when he says that if "*the spy's identity and activities are divulged before the mission is accomplished, then the spy and those who have been told of the matter should be put to death.*"

Those who do not "*pray in secret*" just as the Bible suggests will accept all that their circumstances dictate for they do not know how to turn within themselves to seek for the solution to their problems. They will not be able to experience the *Truth* of the Universal Law from using mental *spies*.

So, turn away from your five external senses and direct them within to visualise that the ideal exists in your current reality the way you wish it to be. There is simply no limit to the purpose that you can *employ* mental *spies* for.

凡軍之所欲擊，城之所欲攻，人之所欲殺；必先知其守將，左右，謁者，門者，舍人之姓名，令吾間必索知之。

Generally, one who wishes to fight the enemy, attack a city or assassinate an individual, it is crucial for our spies to know the exact identities of the defending Generals, attendants, associates, gatekeepers and in-house officers by their names.

This statement by Sun Tzu suggests that one has to be precise and meticulous to detail. If you want to objectify an ideal, you will have to visualise in your mind that the desire has already been fulfilled. It is *crucial* to construct a scene with sharp details that implies its fulfilment to convince your subconscious mind as to the reality of your vision. You must know off-handedly the feeling of the wish fulfilled.

Ask yourself the following questions to define the details to engage your five inner senses to aid your visualisation process:

1) How do you feel now that your wish is already fulfilled?
2) What do you 'see', 'hear', 'smell', 'taste' and 'touch' that imply your desire has already objectified on this physical plane?

The answers to the questions above are essential for anyone who wishes to re-write their current reality to be other than what they are experiencing now.

必索敵間之來間我者，因而利之，導而舍之，故反間可得而使也。

One must be able to identify the enemy's spies who have come to spy on us and tempt them with advantages. Then, direct them and keep them as ours. That is how one can employ a traitor for one's own benefit.

This is exactly what W. Clement Stone means when he says: *"in every adversity, there is a seed for a greater benefit."*

Failures and difficulties are actually blessings in disguise if you adopt the right mental attitude. You must possess a positive mindset in order to turn challenges into advantages. This is what draws the line between a winner and a loser.

因是而知之，故鄉間內間可得而使也；因是而知之，故死間為誑事，可使告敵；因是而知之，故生間可使如期。五間之事，主必知之，知之必在于反間，故反間不可不厚也。

Owing to the traitor's information and knowledge, one is then able to:
1) *Acquire and employ a native spy.*
2) *Employ a 'dead spy' to spread deceiving information to the enemy.*
3) *Ensure that a surviving spy can be used as planned.*

In the matter pertaining to the five types of spies, the Master must realise that one's knowledge and information of the enemy is to be obtained from their traitor. Therefore, they must be treated with utmost generosity.

Since the world exists on the concept of duality, it is through experiencing that which you deem undesirable that you will know what is actually desirable.

Once you have distinguished what you desire to experience in your physical reality from that which you do not, you will then be able to embark on the journey to realise it by employing the mental *spies* that are listed earlier in this chapter.

Therefore, a Master who has complete mastery over the mind will always practice equanimity; he or she will always be calm and treat both good and bad alike. The Master realises that it is through the *knowledge and information* gained from experiencing that which is deemed "negative" that he or she can decide on worthy ideals.

"All luck is good luck to the man who bears it with equanimity." (Ancius Manlius Severinus Boethius)

昔殷之興也，伊摯在夏。周之興也，呂牙在殷。故明君賢將，能以上智為間者，必成大功，此兵之要，三軍之所恃而動也。

In ancient times, the Yin dynasty flourished because of Yi Zhi, who had served the Xia Dynasty. Likewise, the Zhou Dynasty's rise is also owed to Lu Ya, who had served the Yin Dynasty. Therefore, only a wise ruler and a good General are able to use the most intelligent individuals of the army for the purpose of spying, which will lead to successful results. Spies are extremely important in warfare as all three ranks of the army rely on them to execute their plans.

Conclusively, the power of employing mental *spies* to turn unfavourable circumstances into favourable ones cannot be undermined. They play a crucial role in *executing the plans* of manifesting any reality that man desires.

So, employ Rahab today to objectify the desires that are worthy of you. There will come a day when you will realise you are actually employing Rahab all the time; the only difference lies in whether you use her to objectify experiences that you truly desire or those that you do not. The mind of man is a double-edged sword; it can be used to save, yet it can also be used to kill. Therefore, direct the mind wisely and you are sure to be the Master of your fate.

GENEVIEVE TAN SHU THUNG

ABOUT THE AUTHOR

Genevieve Tan Shu Thung (also known as *Sandhya*) is a spiritual guide, inspirational speaker and author. She is well-known for the meditation technique named after her – "*Sandhya Maarga Meditation*". This technique brings about rapid transformation within an individual to realise that the innate consciousness is the cause of every activity within the Universe. It helps align an individual with the natural Universal forces and expand the awareness of the infinite Being within each and everyone to maximize their self-potential in all areas of life.

The author has written many inspirational articles related to the power of right-thought and personal development to motivate all to cultivate confidence in the Self of which physical reality manifests from. She has delivered lectures and speeches around the world pertaining to Mental Science and spirituality, and has disciples of different nationalities.

Also an experienced naturopath, Genevieve is the founder and editor-in-chief for *Holistic Living Annex* (*http://www.holisticlivingannex.com*), a magazine-like website to educate people on how to lead a holistic lifestyle to boost the quality of their health and life experiences to achieve success. Not only does she inspire people to harness the power of the mind through her lectures and writings, Genevieve also extends her spiritual teachings in the performing arts field. Through her productions, she has shared subtle messages concerning the philosophy of life.